THE SYMBOLISMS OF HERALDRY

OR

A TREATISE ON THE MEANINGS AND DERIVATIONS OF ARMORIAL BEARINGS

BY

W. CECIL WADE

"*Yet my attempt is not of presumption to teache, (I myselfe having most need to be taught,) but only to the intent that gentlemen that seeke to knowe all good thinges, and woulde have an entrie into this, may not find here a thing expedient but rather a poor help thereto.*"—LEIGH'S *Accedence of Armorie*, London, 1576.

WITH 95 ILLUSTRATIONS

SECOND EDITION

LONDON

GEORGE REDWAY

1898

"Unto the very points and prickes, here are to be found great misteries."—NICHOLAS FLAMMEL, 1399.

"And if aught else great bards beside
   In sage and solemn tunes have sung,
   Of turneys, and of trophies hung,
   Of forests, and enchantments drear,
   Where more is meant than meets the ear."
                                        —MILTON.

Preface

"Heraldry," 1722; Froissart's "Chronicle," translated by Lord Berners, 1525; Edmonson's "Heraldry," 1780; Dallaway's "Heraldry," 1793; Porney's "Heraldry," 1771; and Brydson's "History of Chivalry," 1786. Amongst other writers to whom I have made occasional reference is Sylvanus Morgan, from whom I have very sparingly drawn.

My aim has been to collect the most striking heraldic symbolisms, to attempt—in the spirit of the old armorists—to reconcile any contradictions as to their application, and also to suggest the probable derivation of some of the more ancient emblems, the origin of which may perhaps have been forgotten by the races or families who still display them.

W. CECIL WADE.

PLYMOUTH, *January* 1898.

PREFACE

THE *Daily News* very recently remarked, " Heraldry
is almost a lost art ; the very rage for old book-
plates shows that it takes its rank amongst anti-
quities"; and though we may not agree with this
writer's remarks in their entirety, certain it is that
the collecting of book-plates has really helped to
revive the taste for heraldic studies, and now seems
to invite the publication of my researches on the
subject of armorial symbols.

Besides the chief modern authorities whom I
have consulted, and whose names are given in the
text, I may mention the following older heraldic
writers whose tomes I have examined and com-
pared : Leigh's "Accedence of Arms," 1576 ; Guillim's
" Heraldry," editions of 1610 and 1632, which in-
clude the chief points to be found in Juliana Berners,
Bosworth, and Sir John Ferne's " Glorie of Gene-
rositie " ; also Peacham's "Compleat Gentleman,"
1626 ; Camden's "Remaines," 1623 ; Nisbet's

"What, is it possible? Why, even my uncle reads Gwillym sometimes of a winter night. Not know the figures of heraldry? Of what could your father be thinking."
—DIANA VERNON, *in "Rob Roy."*

"Upon his surcoat valiant Neville bore
  A *silver saltire* upon martial red;
  A *ladie's sleeve* high spirited Hastings wore;
  Ferrer's his tabard with rich *Vairy* spread,
  Well known in many a match before;
  A *raven* sat on Corbet's armed head;
  And Culpeper in *silver arms* enrailed,
  Bore thereupon a *Bloodie Bend engrailed;*
  The noble Percie in that dreadful day
  With a *Bright Crescent* in his guidhaume came;
  In his *White Cornet* Verdon doth display
  A *Fret of Gules*," &c.
                    —DRAYTON'S *"Barons' War."*

TABLE OF CONTENTS

THE

SYMBOLISMS OF HERALDRY

THE ORIGIN OF ARMORIAL BEARINGS

HERALDRY in its present form, commenced to be
displayed in the early part of the twelfth century,
but many of its figures and symbols were derived
from remote ages, and of these some appear to
have come from Asia Minor or Egypt, and many
others from the early Church. Then came many
symbols from the Crusades and of the military and
civil life of that period. After these came certain
merchants' marks, and figures emblematical of the
arts, agriculture, and the chase. Apparently some
figures were introduced with the sole intent of
shadowing forth the bearer's surname. Tournaments brought into regular heraldry many devices
that had been gloriously borne in those brilliant
pageants, and successful wars contributed numerous
decorations to the personal insignia of the victors.
A later and more learned age derived fresh symbols

from classic story. At first these heraldic bearings
were worn on a surcoat above the armour, and so
portions of the vesture became connected with the
coat of arms, such as the furs of ermine, sable, and
" vair," while the scarf, or guige—that is, the shield-
suspender — became the Bend, and the girdle
became the Fess. All of these figures were trans-
ferred to the shield itself, which is often represented in heraldry bearing its owner's crested
helmet above, and draped around with his mantle.
The above statement in *outline* seems desirable at
this point before examining the subject more
closely in detail.

THE SYMBOLIC SIDE OF HERALDRY

HERALDRY has never ranked among the exact arts and sciences, and its study has been held to be of little value in this eminently practical age, for the only merit that has been grudgingly awarded to it by certain writers, is said by them to lie in its connection with its sister science, genealogy. I have not to deal with the genealogical side of the subject, and I propose to refer chiefly to English or British armory, and only occasionally to glance aside at certain features of foreign heraldry, which in practice differs slightly from our own.

It should be premised in dealing with a subject which has become interwoven with the history and daily life of our race for at least seven centuries, that a number of legendary stories and curious theories will have either to be assimilated in the best manner possible, or to be left unsolved altogether, as being the mere exuberances of Gothic fancy. A good deal of what is now deniable has to be charitably accepted as having been credible and estimable in those unenlightened ages, when the crudest ideas gained acceptance among the highest intellects and foremost heroes of whom the world could boast. Much that is out of keeping with our own age appeals to our *tolerance*, as referring to conditions no longer possible, but faithfully reflecting, as it may, the spirit of the old days. It is only by taking a broad-minded view of the limitations of knowledge in the past, that one can derive pleasure from the study of ancient armory. It is in this light that such studies will ever be dear to those who take an interest in the social life of our ancestors, or who desire to recall in imagination the bright pageantry and chivalry of the gentlemen of England, who, for age after age, were loved at home and respected abroad to such an extent as finds no parallel in the history of any other people.

In the present day our poets and artists often turn the "blazoned page" for subjects for their pen and pencil, and fresh attention has been drawn to the subject of armorial devices by the now popular collection and study of those book-plates which exhibit coats of arms, which were originally engraved and printed for insertion, as marks of ownership, within the covers of favourite volumes. Collectors of book-plates have in the *Ex-Libris*

Journal[1] an excellent medium of communication, and in connection with this subject many cultured minds have been drawn to the study of heraldry, among these being many gifted and gentle ladies and gallant young men, who worthily inherit the insignia of the Chivalric Ages, which were never one-tenth so noble, so cultured, or so endurable, as our own more favoured though less picturesque times. Never before the glorious reign of Victoria have humanity, charity, courtesy, and knowledge been so manifest and so widely diffused!

It is held by some that heraldry, or the bearing of arms, is so intimately connected with a patrician aristocracy, that it has no connection with a democratic age or nation. Provided that any democratic nation decided to sever from itself all its traditions and history such might be the case, but that this eventuality has never yet arisen, is proved by the fact that armorial ensigns are still to be found in use in the United States, and in the smaller American republics, as well as in those of France and Switzerland. The first Napoleon introduced a good deal of common-sense procedure in the granting of arms to his followers, and in which it may be remarked that symbolism was never neglected. As

[1] Ably edited by Mr. W. H. K. Wright, Honorary Secretary of the Ex-Libris Society.

some of the most striking and most ancient coats of arms in this country have been, and still are, borne by families which are neither distinguished by titles nor by the possession of particular wealth, heraldry cannot, in England, be said to be an exclusive distinction of the aristocracy. Heraldry seems particularly to pertain, to-day, to the possessors of poetic or artistic temperaments, and to the young, and it is to assist such ardent spirits that this little work is specially devoted. It is not a glossary of the science. Excellent grammars of heraldry are obtainable by any student.

The question is very often asked, Is there any particular meaning in the figures shown in the coat of arms ?

To deal with this query is the first duty of this treatise. Almost every one possesses the idea that the figures of heraldry are, or ought to be, symbolical, and up to a recent date they were generally so received by all the chief writers who have made any reference to the subject. Some doubt, however, has been imported into the question by a work entitled " The Pursuivant of Arms ; or, Heraldry Founded upon Facts," by the late Mr. J. R. Planché, F.S.A., Somerset Herald, a book which, having gone through various editions, has received a good deal of well-deserved attention.

While giving Mr. Planché full credit for all his painstaking labours in various fields of antiquarian research, and for recording many important heraldic facts, one cannot help feeling that in one respect he has permitted his fancy to run away with his judgment, to the extent of believing and saying that "arms took their origin from the desire of certain first assumers to pun on their own names by devices or rebuses, or otherwise simply to express their official dignities and genealogical derivations." He seems to have forgotten that coats of arms were in general use long before surnames became fixed ; and it may be remarked that names and words are themselves often symbols, whilst the earliest form of writing was nothing but a methodised symbolism. He further asserts that many of the principal objects borne in arms were only the "accidental bosses and strengthening pieces which were affixed to the warriors' shields at the period when regular heraldry first arose." Mr. Planché had evidently forgotten, too, that heraldic bearings on "coats of arms" were first actually worn as garments, and were only repeated upon the shield and banner. Speaking of the assumption of arms, he says, "That in their assumption the object of the assumers was, not as it has been so generally asserted and believed,

B

to record any achievement or to symbolise any virtue or qualification, but simply to distinguish their persons and properties; to display their pretensions to certain honours and estates, attest their alliances, or acknowledge their feudal tenures."

I shall endeavour to maintain that true symbolism is often to be found in arms of the earliest period, and that many arms of the same date bore no references to the names or offices of their assumers, and were evidently not adopted as strengthening parts of the shield. On the other hand, it must be admitted that there exist a large number of ancient arms which do exhibit a distinct reference to the names or offices of their owners, and such examples of "canting arms," or "armes parlantes," are well known to every one who has given close attention to heraldry. Examples of this kind of arms are so frequently to be met with that it is unnecessary to refer to many of them here, but their number would seem, at first sight, almost to justify Mr. Planché in his very sweeping assertions. Bearing in mind that arms were at first all self-assumed, and not granted by any authority, it is not surprising to find that some men whose names had shone like stars in a firmament of glory, as well as those who had no particular sentiment or deed to commemorate, should have preferred to symbolise their own names rather than anything else. In just the same way some manufacturers to-day prefer to register their names as trade marks, rather than to assume any distinctive devices. It may by some persons be questioned, if he who punned on his own name in his heraldic bearings was possessed of the highest chivalric sentiment, although, doubtless, he was accepted as the " practical common-sense " man of his age. It should be remarked that canting arms are still borne by many very distinguished families (some of these bearings being among the most ancient on record), and it is important to note that the colours of heraldry, as well as its figures, were held to be symbolical, so that these canting arms are obviously not devoid of heraldic emphatic sentiment. To briefly return again to Mr. Planché's theories, it may be remarked that he tacitly admits in his popular work, that the following bearings were imported into heraldry as tokens of the Crusades, which commenced almost simultaneously with the rise of heraldry itself —namely, crosses of various kinds, crescents, pilgrims' staves and water-bottles, escallop shells— which were the ancient badges of pilgrims— bezants or coins of gold, annulets or rings, swords, battle-axes, and arrow-heads. If, then, he accepts these objects as having been imported into arms

with a symbolical intention from the dawn of
heraldry, what becomes of his previous very posi-
tive assertions as to the absence of any such
intent? Amongst the ancient arms which he
quotes, he has given two examples of coats which
he found in a roll of the thirteenth century, and
these on examination will, I think, scarcely support
his views. They are as follows : John de la Hay
bore on a silver shield a red sun in its splendour,
and Rauf de la Hay, his brother, bore a silver
shield with one red ray of the sun. He has not
troubled himself to show in what manner these
very early bearings typified the offices of their
bearers, and he could hardly claim the RAY of
the sun as meaning R. de la Hay, because to do
so would be to leave John de la Hay with his entire
sun eclipsed, from a punster's point of view ! It
is evident that both of these are highly symbolical
bearings, and have no reference to their owners'
names, offices, or alliances.

I have been compelled to make these references
to Mr. Planché's work, because he was not only a
high antiquarian authority, but also a distinguished
herald attached to the College of Arms, and his
work has received a great deal of attention from
all students of heraldry, while the statements referred to prove that he is not an infallible guide

on this subject. So far is it from being the case
that there was ever a general desire to pun on
their own names, on the part of the original
assumers of coats of arms, that it may be definitely
stated that regular armorial bearings were in general
use throughout Europe long before the surname
became fixed as an invariable adjunct to each
branch or generation of the same family. There
is also proof extant that some worthy knights
assumed cognomens suggested by their own armorial devices.

Is heraldry then symbolical? It would have
been deemed quite unnecessary to have asked this
question seventy or eighty years ago, when Sir
Walter Scott,—who was the most deeply read
scholar in mediæval lore that literature has ever
owned,—in his novels and poems, drew the attention of the world, to the deep and dignified symbolisms which lay hidden beneath the devices
and neglected escutcheons of our ancient families.
Scott makes many beautiful and striking allusions
to the emblematical side of heraldry throughout
his works. Chaucer, Shakespeare, Spenser, and
Sidney also afford many poetic references to the
symbols of heraldry, and we may safely assume
that they all faithfully reflect the culture and knowledge of the periods in which they lived. Although,

by common consent, heraldry, or the regular bearing of coats of arms, or garments bearing symbols,
cannot be traced before the period of the Crusades,
the custom of bearing various symbols on shields,
helmets, and ensigns or standards, extended to the
remotest antiquity. It is probable that to ancient
Egypt—the birthplace apparently of all the arts
and sciences—may be ascribed the first use of
symbols. Dr. John Macdonell in his recent elo-
quent lectures before the Royal Institution on
"Symbolism in Ceremonies, Customs, and Art,"
ably defined the original use of symbols as having
been to supplement defects in language before
writing was generally practised. "Some symbolisms," he remarks, "like some phrases, have
travelled all over the world, and are to be met with
in varying climes. As there were dead languages,
so there are dead symbols and ceremonies handed
down, whose tradition and origin are unknown.
Words having a sacred association, as a rule, have
escaped mutation. The same held good with the
sacred symbols, the Crescent as a symbol of one
faith, and the Cross of another, having for many
centuries preserved their precise significance. The
coronation service or ceremonial is a complex
service of imitations of acts usual, and even necessary, in times when the king was the captain of his

people." He concluded one of his lectures by referring to the vastness of the whole subject of symbolism, "which began and ended only where life itself began and ended."

We read of the Lion borne as an ensign of the tribe of Judah, the Eagle of the Romans, the two-headed Eagle of the East—still borne by two great European Empires ; of the White Horse of Wodin, borne by Hengist when he invaded Britain—which the shield of Hanover still bears ; of the Raven, borne by the ancient Danes ; of the Crescent and Star, borne by the followers of Mahomet, and now retained by the Turkish Empire as its national device.

It is to the time of the earlier Crusades, in the early part of the twelfth century, that we can ascribe the establishment of armorial bearings in their present form, when the necessity of quickly recognising each of the numerous leaders seems to have compelled the princes and knights to adopt a methodical arrangement of various distinguishing devices, borne on surcoat and banner, and at first by them only occasionally displayed upon the shield itself. It was not until the reign of Henry III. that such bearings became hereditary. There is no account extant of the particular usages connected with the first adoption of heraldic devices. Indeed,

the first work in English on this subject did not
appear until 1485, when Wynkin de Worde printed
the Book of St. Albans, in which Dame Juliana
Berners had translated an earlier work, on what she
calls "Cote Armuris," from the Latin, by Nicholas
Upton, Canon of Salisbury. This lady states em-
phatically, that arms were at first all assumed by
their bearers, without heralds or other authority,
and she considers such arms as good as those
granted by the heralds themselves. Heralds' College
was only constituted in the reign of Richard III.,
in 1483, so that the foundations of heraldry were
established in the arbitrary assumptions of arms by
various individuals. It arises from the fact that
there was at first no authority to regulate the bearing of arms, that so much uncertainty surrounds the
whole subject, and that so many different opinions
have to be examined and, if it be possible, recon-
ciled. We find in connection with many ancient
crests and coats of arms, a number of surprising
or incongruous objects, which defy modern heralds
to explain them satisfactorily, and the legendary
origins of which have become shrouded by the
mists of many ages. Dallaway, writing on this
subject, says, "Certain it is that many of the oldest
families in Wales bear what may be termed legendary pictures having little or no analogy to the

more systematic armory of England; such, for instance, as a wolf issuing from a cave; a cradle under a tree with a child guarded by a goat, &c." The most simple coats of arms are usually the most ancient, while some comparatively modern grants of arms are so confused as to convey no particular meanings, and have been justly derided for their "marine views and miniature landscapes," which would require a microscope to do them justice! These pictorial arms were chiefly the introductions of heralds of the last century, of whom many professed, and possessed, little antiquarian knowledge or respect for the traditions of their ancient and historic office. On the other hand, we have thousands of examples of ancient coats of arms that contain a clear symbolic expression, through either the figures or the colours which they display. The colours of heraldry were held to be symbolical by all the old heraldic writers, and the best authorities of different periods are generally fairly agreed as to the chief symbolism to be attributed to each colour. Every one from his or her childhood has been accustomed to associate certain ideas with particular colours, and these associations generally concur with the heraldic rules regarding them. For instance, blue is the colour of loyalty and truth; white, or silver, goes for peace and sincerity; black

is for constancy and grief; yellow or gold is for
generosity and elevation of mind; green agrees
with the springtime and with hope; red, with
martial fortitude and magnanimity; and purple is
the colour of sovereign majesty and justice. The
heraldic beasts, such as the dragon, wyvern, griffin,
and unicorn, have been the objects of a good deal
of satire on the part of those who have industriously
set about crying down the Middle Age and all its
works and devices. It has, however, been held
by some writers that the dragon and wyvern are
really the legendary reproductions of the crocodile,
and that the unicorn was really the rhinoceros.
About these animals oral traditions may have been
handed down from that remote age, when such
creatures were the terror of those Eastern lands in
which we are led to believe our race first dwelt.
The Bible makes frequent reference to dragons,
unicorns, and fiery flaming serpents—in a symbolical sense only—showing that these creatures
existed in the popular imagination at a very early
period. We can very readily believe that the
earlier races of mankind, armed as they were with
only simple weapons of stone or bronze, would
have been almost powerless to resist the approach
of a crocodile or of a rhinoceros, or even to pre-
vent the descent of an eagle; so it might come to

pass that a devastation inflicted on their flocks, or
perhaps the loss of beloved children, would cause
the powerful destroyer to become magnified by
tradition to something still more fearful and wonderful. The forces of nature were also dreaded
to an incredible extent by our ancestors, and
comets, meteors, and the appearance of an aurora,
were freely accepted as certain harbingers of
disaster to the world! We should remember
these quaint old-world conditions when we regard
the fabulous creatures preserved in heraldry, or
read of the alleged awful phenomena of nature,
gravely recorded in old histories, of which a curious
collection might be formed.

I have referred to the fabulous beasts alluded to
in the Scriptures, and it should here be added that
heraldry itself is full of emblematical bearings which
refer to sacred subjects. This side of heraldry
has been singularly overlooked. There can be no
doubt that to the portrayal of some religious sentiment, or reference to some particular passage in
Scripture that had been found helpful in time of
trial, may be ascribed a large number of the
armorial bearings to be found throughout Europe.
The frequent bearing of objects in threes, in memory
of the Trinity,—the Cross and the Crucifix, the
chalice, the Sacred Heart, the Virgin, the cruci-

fixion nails, the single Star of Bethlehem, or "the Morning Star"—and a number of other similar objects, are readily to be met with wherever one turns. German heraldry appears to offer an unusual number of examples of arms which are allusive to religious subjects. Additional interest is lent to the collection of book-plates or *Ex-Libris*, by the surprising variety of armorial devices which are to be met with among the more ancient, and especially the foreign, specimens. Scotch armory, too, is full of symbolism. The Scotch at first closely followed the French heralds, being much associated with them during the Scottish monarchy.

It is in many cases difficult to assign the exact reason for the original assumption of a particular coat of arms. In the case of any ancient family, in order to arrive at the actual or even a presumptive reason, it would be necessary to study the early history, traditions, and feudal associations of such family. In the instances of those arms that were anciently granted to families by Heralds' College, we know that among the early heralds certain rules were followed, but these were rather jealously guarded, and it is only here and there in their published writings that they refer darkly to the "secrets of heralds."

Several years ago in a sale-room I met with the

printed works of an English herald, in which he stated the practical reasons which had influenced him in granting various new coats of arms. I permitted the name of the work to escape unnoted, and have since vainly queried as to the author among my heraldic friends. I do not refer to the quaint suggestions of Gerard Leigh in his "Accedence of Arms."

As an instance of the manufacture of legends to account for particular bearings, we have the story, repeated even by the illustrious Camden, as to the origin of the arms of Godfrey de Bouillon, who bore three alerions, or small eagles without feet or beaks. The story goes, that when at Jerusalem he "with one draught of his bow broched three feetless birds upon his arrow, and therefore assumed the three birds in his shield." Planché amusingly remarks, "It is impossible now to ascertain who *broached* this wonderful story, but it is perfectly evident that it was the narrator who drew the longbow, and not the noble Godfrey." Putting aside this mediæval fable, we here come to the interesting fact that it is at this period, about A.D. 1100, that we find the first undoubtedly symbolical shield of arms. When Godfrey de Bouillon was selected by the Crusaders as their first king of Jerusalem, he assumed a coat of arms which was borne by that kingdom during its short existence of less than a century,

and that is still to be found borne on various
modern escutcheons. It is interesting to note that
this coat, being one of the very earliest, is a symbolical one, and further, that it is admitted to be so by
Mr. Planché himself! It consists of a silver shield,
in the centre of which is a large Cross Potent (a
cross with crutch-shaped ends), surrounded by four
smaller plain crosses. All the crosses are of gold.
Here we have the Crusaders founding a kingdom of
their own, and what more appropriate device could
they exhibit than that very cross for which they had
striven ? The number of the crosses refers to that
of the chief nations then engaged in the war. Mr.
Lower, in his intensely interesting " Curiosities of
Heraldry," says that he thinks that stags, deer, wolves,
boars, foxes, and dogs are probably emblems of the
chase. I venture to think that the adoption of such
objects often had a more symbolical purpose than
the mere pictorial reference to that everyday employment of almost all men in the Middle Ages, when
literature and scientific studies were almost unknown, and when politics did not offer a tempting,
or even a safe, employment. It would not be difficult
to find from passages of Scripture, or incidents
in the pages of history, excellent reasons why
these emblems may have been specially adopted
by their assumers, and subsequently proudly borne

by their descendants. The bearing of animals is undoubtedly one of the most ancient forms of symbolism. The lion, lamb, and hart are often admiringly spoken of in the Old Testament. The wolf was a sacred emblem in Egypt, and Lycopolis was named after it, because of the worship offered to it in that city. A wolf was also one of the oldest military ensigns of Rome, in reference to the fabulous history of the origin of the city. The boar's head was often the fee mentioned as due to the king, or to the great lord, as the condition of feudal tenure, and its introduction in Queen's College, Oxford, in connection with the well-known Christmas festivities, certainly never had any reference to the chase, but points rather to the meaning ascribed to it by some old heralds, who say that the boar's head is the token of hospitality. It is brought into the dining-hall with the song :

Boar's head couped.

> " The boar's head, I understand,
>   Is the chief service in this land;
>   And look wherever it be found,
>   Servite cum cantico."

This carol was printed by Wynkin de Worde in 1521.

Speaking of such singular devices as three-headed

or three-tailed lions, Mr. Lower says, " It would be a mere waste of time to speculate on the origin of such fantastic bearings." He however held that, as a whole, heraldry was symbolical in its intent, and he gives a number of symbolisms, some of which are to be found in this treatise. Lower's " Curiosities of Heraldry" is now rarely to be met with, having been out of print for many years.

In another part of this essay I have referred to the various plans which have been observed from time to time in order to " difference" or distinguish between the various branches of one family, by means of more or less important alterations in their armorial bearings, or else in the colours of their various shields. It is unnecessary for me to do more than mention those special " Augmentations" or additions of honour, which have been granted by British and foreign sovereigns, in order to specially distinguish their subjects, for signal actions of loyalty or valour. It seems to be a pity that this practice has now fallen into disuse, and that decorations are merely bestowed on the hero's *coat* instead of upon his ancestral coat of arms! Augmentations of arms are constantly to be met with in various works which are known to all heraldic students.

Heraldry offers as a subject of study many

things that are rational and full of interest, besides being in itself so closely interwoven with the inner lives of our countrymen who lived in the stirring times when the name and power of England were both "in the making." The glorious period of heraldry has passed for ever, but its bright and gilded old escutcheons ever appeal to the poetic and artistic tastes of the youth of both sexes, who find as they grow older, that the glamour and fascination of these beautiful memorials of the past, are not destroyed by life's vivid or dull realities.

Mr. Lower in his "Curiosities of Heraldry," eloquently speaking of the palmy days of heraldry, says, "Then were the banners and escutcheons of war refulgent with blazon, the light of every chancel and hall was stained with the tinctures of heraldry, the tiled pavement vied with the fretted roof, every corbel, every vane spoke proudly of the battlefield, and filled every breast with a lofty emulation of the deeds which earned such stately rewards. We, the men of this prosaic nineteenth century, have, it is probable, but a faint idea of the influence which heraldry exerted in the minds of our rude forefathers of that chivalric age." To this I would like to add, that symbolism, both in the Church and in everyday life and literature,

C

formed the vital force that animated our ancestors
in thought and action, in a period full of both sentiment and theatrical display, and unless we bear this
fact in mind, we shall fail to form a just idea of the
lives and deeds of the chief actors in the stirring
dramas of ancient times.

If heraldry may be said to be in one sense a
survival of the ages of the deluded alchymist and
astrologer, and of the witch and heretic hunter, it
is also a memorial of the brave and true hearts and
great names, of those really downright-in-earnest
and picturesque times, and a monument to the
men who, by their energy, love of liberty, and
valour, very largely contributed to make this realm
what it is for us to-day. It therefore follows that
while armorial bearings are interesting relics of
bygone men and times, they also now form fitting
ornaments, full of rich associations, for an historic
people like our own.

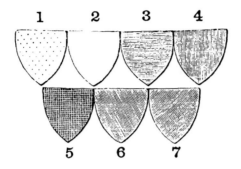

HERALDIC COLOURS AND METALS

THE following definitions of armorial colours will be found to agree with those of the majority of the leading authorities :—

OR, yellow or gold. No. 1.—Called Jaune by some old writers, is represented in engravings by dots. It denoted Generosity and, according to Sir John Ferne, Elevation of Mind. This and the next colour represent the two Metals of Heraldry.

ARGENT, white or silver. No. 2.—Represented in engraving by a white space, unless a "diaper" pattern be introduced for the purpose of adding to the effect. Signifies Peace and Sincerity.

SABLE, or black. No. 5.—Represented in engraving by closely crossed lines or by a deep black. Denotes Constancy, and sometimes, but more rarely, Grief.

AZURE, or blue. No. 3.—Represented in engraving by horizontal lines. Signifies Loyalty and Truth. It was the colour devoted to the Virgin by the Roman Church.

GULES, or red. No. 4.—Represented by perpendicular lines. Denotes Military Fortitude and Magnanimity. It is also "the martyr's colour."

VERT, or green. No. 6.—Represented in engraving by oblique lines from the dexter or right corner of the shield * to the sinister base, or left lower part. Signifies Hope, Joy, and, sometimes, Loyalty in Love.

PURPURE, purple. No. 7.—Represented in engraving by diagonal lines from the sinister or left corner to the dexter base. Denotes Royal Majesty, Sovereignty, and Justice. It is called by the old heralds the most majestical of colours.

TENNE or TAWNEY, or orange colour, sometimes by old heralds called Brusque, is little used in British heraldry. In engravings it is represented by lines from the sinister chief to the dexter base, crossed by horizontal lines. It was said to signify "Worthy Ambition."

MURRAY, or sanguine. This, like Tawney, was seldom used in English coats of arms, but both

---

* The dexter side of the shield is really the left side as one looks at it, being on its bearer's right.

have often been used as party or livery colours. It is represented in engraving by diagonal lines crossing each other. The meaning of this has been stated by Leigh to be "Not hasty in battle, and yet a victor."

Murray, or sanguine.

The old heralds used to say when a coat of arms bore only black and white it was "most fair," when black and gold it was "most rich," but when of green and gold it was "most glorious." Although argent is frequently depicted in its proper colour of silver, it is more generally borne of a plain white colour, and this is due to the fact, as Robson points out in his useful work on heraldry, that silver will quickly become tarnished and turn black.

For the purpose of giving greater prominence to heraldic bearings, the rule has been generally adhered to, that colour should not be borne upon colour, nor metal upon metal. The various furs ranked according to their colours in applying this rule, excepting the compound-coloured furs, which were treated like metals.

THE FURS OF HERALDRY

THE FURS of heraldry are borne of various colours, and in each instance would have the particular signification attached to its colour, in addition to the fact that the wearing of fur, in ancient days, was considered a particular mark of dignity, and such would not have formed part of "the coat" of any person of an inferior degree in rank. We are told that when Innocent III. granted absolution to Henry of Falconburg, who was accessory to the murder of Conrad, the first Bishop of Würzburg, he enjoined on him as a penance, that he should fight against the Saracens, but was never to appear in Ermine or Vair, or in any other armorial

Vair.

colours made use of in tournaments. I need only make one or two further remarks on this subject. The fur called Vair, which is represented by lines of bell-shaped objects, generally of blue alternating with white, is said to be the skin of an animal of the weasel kind, named *Varus*, which was once used for the lining of military cloaks. It is stated by old heralds that it was first brought into armory because Signor de Cancis, when fighting in Hungary, succeeded in rallying his retreating army by displaying his Vair cloak, and thenceforward adopted it as the ensign of his signory. Another compound-coloured fur, something like Vair, is called Potent. It is composed of figures shaped like the ends of a crutch, arranged in rows, and of alternate colours.

ERMINE has so long been associated with the robes and crowns of royal and noble personages, that it is easy to under- stand why it should be considered as a perfect emblem of dignity in any *coat* of arms. It is probable that the colour black or sable was first found

Ermine.

on the actual sur-coat in the shape of a fur. Fur is still worn on the hoods of collegiate graduates *as a bearing of honour*.

Ermines. Is a black fur with white spots.

Erminois. Is yellow with black spots.

Pean. Is black with yellow spots. But the above are of rare occurrence.

THE MEANING OF HERALDIC LINES

THE following lines are used in armory, in addition to straight lines :—

The Nebulée or Nebuly line denotes clouds or air :

The Undée or Wavy line represents the sea or water, and is represented in two ways :

The engrailed and invecked lines signify earth or land :

Engrailed.

Invecked.

The indented represents fire :

Dancetté is also attributed to mean water :

Ragulée or Raguly signifies difficulties which have been encountered :

The above are Guillim's definitions, but he holds that the Embattled line, here shown, is also an

emblem of fire, but it will be found that Nisbet and all the other ancient authorities state that it denotes the walls of a fortress or town. Guillim has made several remarks on the subject of these lines, which it is unnecessary for us to follow. It is difficult now to surmise the chief reasons for the assignment of some of these lines by the ancient heralds. Guillim remarks that behind the use of many of these "flecked lines" *lie hidden some of the many secrets of heralds.* It is a pity that he was not a little more lucid while on this subject. Sir Harris Nicolas, in his "Memoir of Augustine Vincent, Windsor Herald," speaks of the modern practice

in granting arms as being "too frequently radiant
in hieroglyphical allusions to the trade by which
the obscure parvenue has just emerged from in-
significance." This is another allusion to the
secrets of heralds! It is difficult to agree with
Sir Harris Nicolas as to such practice having been
frequently adopted by modern heralds. Examples
of such grants are certainly "far to seek."

Grants of arms are now obtainable from the
Colleges of Arms in London, Edinburgh, and
Dublin, and such grants are devised by the heralds
on highly rational principles, employing many of
the symbolisms noted in this essay.

THE SYMBOLISMS OF THE ORDINARIES

THE colour of the Ordinary was held to be symbolical, as well as the colour of the field or ground of the escutcheon. The first in importance is called a "Chief," which, as it occupies the whole of the top and one-third of the total surface of the shield of arms, is the best position in which any device can be represented — unless we except the most central point of the escutcheon. It is said to signify Dominion and Authority, and it has often been granted as a special reward for prudence and wisdom, as well as for successful command in war.

A chief Or (gold), bearing three swans' heads erased, and in base a castle on a mount "proper," on a field azure.

The large plain cross is another of the so-called "Honourable Ordinaries." This was first adopted in general heraldic use by those who had actually served in the Crusades. The smaller crosses borne in coats of arms are not considered to be Ordinaries, but simple charges. When the Cross was

Cross fleurettée.

borne "Flory" or "Fleurettée," *i.e.* flowered at each end, it was held to signify one who had conquered, but when borne "Raguly," *i.e.* drawn with lines Ragulée, it denoted that very great difficulty had been encountered. (Guillim.)

The Cross Patoncée or Cross Flory is a somewhat frequent bearing, and means the

Cross patoncée or cross flory.

same as the fleurettée cross. The above are generally only borne as "Ordinaries," but other forms of crosses, excepting Saltires, are usually borne as common charges. The Cross, says dear old Guillim, is the most honourable charge to be found in heraldry, and its bearing is the express badge of the Christian. "All crosses signify unto us tribulation and affliction."

The large crosses are also borne engrailed, invecked, &c., while as common charges they are found borne in arms in a variety of forms, which

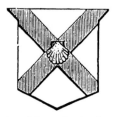
A saltire gules (red) bearing an escallop Or (gold).

may be found depicted in most heraldic text-books. In heraldry every form of the Cross had a direct reference to the Church and its Risen Head.

The SALTIRE or St. Andrew's Cross, which is another of the Ordinaries, is the symbol of Resolution, and Guillim says it was the reward of such as have scaled the walls of towns. The Saltire crossed at each point is called a St. Julian's Cross.

The CHEVRON signifies Protection, and has often been granted in arms as a reward to one who has achieved some notable enterprise. It is supposed to represent the roof-tree of a house, and

A chevron gules (red) on a shield Or (gold).

A chevronel azure (blue) on a shield argent (silver).

has sometimes been given to those who have built churches or fortresses, or who have accomplished some work of faithful service. CHEVRONELS are small chevrons, and these are the military stripes of merit worn by our gallant soldiers and sailors.

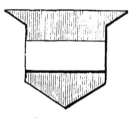

A fess argent on a shield gules.

The FESS, or band borne in the centre of the shield, is the military belt or girdle of honour.

The BAR is of the same form as the Fess, but of lesser breadth. It is said by Guillim to be suitable

as a bearing for one "who sets the bar of conscience, religion, and honour against angry passions

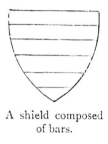

A shield composed
of bars.

Barrulet.

and evil temptations."   The same significance
would be given to the BARRULET, which is again
less than the Bar.

Speaking of the Fess, Guillim says, "It is a
military girdle of honour, and signifies that the
bearer must be always in readiness to undergo the
business of the public weal."   Upton, speaking of
the bearing of a Bar Nebulée, *i.e.* formed with the
Cloud lines (page 40), says, it denotes some high
excellence in its first bearer.   Of the bearing of
"Barry Wavy," *i.e.* bars composed of the waved
lines, Guillim says, "They may put us in mind that
as in a tempestuous storm one wave succeeds high
above the other in immediate succession, so God
has ordained that one trouble should succeed
another to keep His chosen in continual exercise,
and that His faithful may have manifold experience of His great providence and Fatherly care in

preserving them in all their troubles, giving them a comfortable event and happy end in all their afflictions."

As an example of the symbolic bearing of the wavy Fess, we read that Sir Francis Drake had granted to him, on a black shield, a Fess Wavy between two polestars—the Arctic and Antarctic—all coloured silver or white. The crest was a sphere, around which a ship is depicted being drawn by a hand issuing from the clouds. This coat of arms, it is stated by Peacham, was especially devised for him by Queen Elizabeth herself, and in every way it refers to Drake's great achievement in sailing around the world. The very colours were symbolical of Constancy and Peace, besides their consisting of the pure blend of black and white, which the old heralds held to signify "Fame." I have omitted from this treatise a list of the rather contradictory theories of the old heralds which I had collected, respecting the significance of the pure blending of any two of the various colours or metals.

A pale, charged with a sword.

The PALE is said to denote Military Strength and Fortitude, and has been bestowed on those who have impaled or otherwise defended cities, or who have supported the government of their sovereigns, and, "for standing uprightly to their prince and country." (Guillim.)

The PALET is a diminutive of the Pale, and the ENDORSE is a still further diminutive of the Palet, and would in each case signify the same as the Pale.

The PILE is supposed to represent the large pieces of wood used by engineers in the construc-

A pile bearing three stars of six points between six stars.

tion of bridges, or of buildings on insecure or marshy ground. It is therefore well fitted, Guillim states, for an engineer or for one who has shown great ability in any kind of construction. It has also occasionally been adopted as a "difference" in the arms of members of one family. When only one pile is found borne on a shield it very much resembles a pennon or small pointed flag, and it may be that this was intended when only one is represented.

The CANTON stands very high among honourable bearings. Like all the other "Ordinaries," it is sometimes found borne plain, and at other times with charges on it, and it may be said to be like a flag introduced at the top corner of the shield. When it is borne charged it often contains some special symbols granted by the sovereign in reward for the performance of eminent service. Of this kind of reward many ancient ex-amples are to be found in our own and other countries.

Arms of Shakespeare. The shield is Or (gold), and on a bend sable a lance of the first colour. Crest, an eagle holding a lance.

The QUARTER is as large again as the Canton, and occupies exactly one-quarter of the shield. This has also at times been directly granted, charged with special bearings, as a reward from the sovereign for brilliant military service. It is considered, says Francis Nichols in his "British Compendium of Heraldry," in the light of a banner specially con-ferred.

The BEND is also a bearing of high honour, and probably re-presents either the scarf or the shield suspender of a knight or military commander. (See arms of Shakespeare.) It is held to signify Defence or Protection. It was, like most other bearings, at first assumed by men of knightly and military rank, and it has since often been granted by the heralds to those who have distinguished themselves as commanders.

D

The diminutive of the Bend Dexter is the BEND-

LET. A still further diminutive of the Bend is the COST, which is usually borne in couples, and then called Cotises. These often enclose or protect the Bend, which is then said to be "cotized." When a bend or bendlet is borne placed above a lion or other similar charge, the latter is said to be "debruised by such bend or bendlet."

A bendlet ermine debruising a lion rampant.

The RIBBON is still less than the cost, and, according to Nisbet, was borne by Abernethy as follows : On a gold shield, a red lion rampant, surmounted by a black ribbon. I have slightly translated the heraldic language for the convenience of the reader, and shall here generally follow this course. The Ribbon, like the maunche or lady's sleeve, was probably a tournament *gage d'amour*, and thence adopted into heraldry.

The Bend Sinister is equally as honourable as the Bend Dexter, as also is the "Scarfe," or diminutive of the bend sinister, which latter is also the "badge of honour for a commander." A great many people who have paid no attention to heraldry speak of "the bend sinister" as though it meant the mark of illegitimacy, but it is really nothing of the kind.

The BATTUNE SINISTER, or baton shortened at
each end, has often been, and is still,
used as marking a royal descent that
is barred by illegitimacy from succession to the throne. In ancient times
other heraldic devices were sometimes employed to express the same
meaning.

Stuart Royal Arms
with battune sinis-
ter.

The ORLE or TRESSURE is classed as
an "Ordinary," and is considered to be a diminutive
of the Border. It is borne in the arms of Scotland,
and was held to be the emblem of Preservation or
Protection. It is needless to credit the legend as to
this tressure having been anciently given to Achaius,

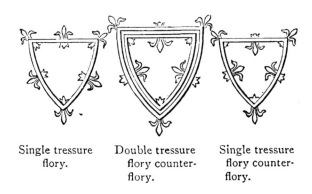

| Single tressure flory. | Double tressure flory counter-flory. | Single tressure flory counter-flory. |

King of Scots, by Charlemagne, in order to signify
that the French lilies should defend the Scottish lion.
Porny says that the DOUBLE tressure in the arms
of Scotland was first assumed by Robert Stuart, to
testify his approval of the alliance which he had

renewed with King Charles V. of France. We may well doubt the reference to Charlemagne, but there

is little reason to doubt that the tressure "fleury counter-fleury" was adopted by one of the Scottish kings to commemorate that close alliance which existed between France and Scotland for so many ages. Some-

Roses borne in orle with an inescutcheon.

times charges are borne around the shield in the form of an Orle, when they are described as being "in Orle."

FLASQUES. This reward, says Leigh in his "Accedence of Armory," is to be given by a king for virtue and learning, and especially for service in embassage. FLANCHES, Leigh considers to be a degree under Flasques, yet, says he, are they commendable armory. Nisbet considers both these figures to be really the same as Voiders.

VOIDERS. Such, remarks Leigh, are given to gentlewomen who have deserved highly. In the arms granted by Henry VIII. to his wife Katharine Howard, we have an example of this bearing. Her specially granted arms were, a blue shield, on which were three golden fleur-de-lis between two ermine voiders each charged with a red rose.

The BORDURE or Border is another "Ordinary."

This form of bearing is of great antiquity, and was frequently adopted as a "difference" between relatives bearing the same arms. In other cases it was used as an augmentation of honour.

A border engrailed, and a Maltese cross.

The INESCUTCHEON. This is seldom found borne as an Ordinary, being generally a coat of arms borne as an escutcheon of Pretence, superimposed upon a shield of arms, in testimony of the claim of a prince to the sovereignty of the country so repre-sented, or if by a private personage, then as the sign that he had married the heiress of the family indicated, and that their joint descendants might sub-sequently claim to quarter these arms with their own. In the annexed arms

Arms of William III and Queen Mary.

of William III. the inescutcheon gives the arms of Holland. With regard to the custom of quartering, there appears to be little reason for this practice, ex-cepting where there is a union of kingdoms, or when an additional surname has been assumed. "Let each man bear his own arms and none other," is an old saying! It is interesting to see a "many quartered coat" in a hall or library, or in a book-plate, where the minutiæ can be carefully delineated and easily deciphered, but the public display of such coats of many colours savours somewhat of vanity, or at least is very confusing.

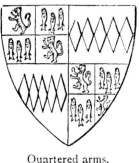

Quartered arms.

Plantagenet and
Tudor royal arms.

The Gyron has been considered an "Ordinary." Some modern writers have objected to the term  Ordinary as being an unnecessary classification, but it has now become useful when consulting that excellent dictionary called "Papworth's Ordinary of Arms," which is arranged for reference purposes under the various

A gyron.

ordinaries and colours found in a coat of arms. By this means the names of the owners of many escutcheons on plate, pictures, or un-named bookplates may be discovered. The Gyron is said to be typical of Unity. It is never borne singly, but two or more occupy a large portion of the shield. The Campbells bear Gyrons in their arms, as also do many other families.

THE DIVISION LINES OF THE SHIELD

WHEN a coat of arms is divided by an oblique line, it is termed parti *per* Bend, because the line is the same as that of the bend. If a shield be borne divided by a horizontal line, it is called parti *per* Fess. If there be a perpendicular line in the centre of the shield, it is parted "*per* Pale." The same rule applies to lines in the form of a Saltire or Cross, only in the latter case the lines may be caused by the conjunction of four coats in one shield, when the term employed would be " quarterly," and not " per Cross."

If there are several bend-shaped lines, the term applied is " Bendy of so many pieces," distinguishing the alternate colours, commencing with the first metal or colour at the Dexter or left-hand highest corner of the shield as it faces the spectator. If there are several Bar or Fess-like lines, then it should be called "Barry of so many pieces," naming the colours, commencing with the colour at the top of the shield. If the lines are perpendicular, it is called "paley," and the colours must be described commencing from the Dexter or left side of the shield as it faces the one who views it. The

SINISTER side is always that which appears at the right of the shield as one faces it, because this would really be the sinister or left side of its bearer.

The object in parting a shield by the various lines, seems to have been to thereby employ two colours conspicuously either as symbolic or livery colours. Many examples of arms are to be found which bear simply two colours parted by one or more lines. Unless the symbolism of the colours be recognised, such arms would be perfectly meaningless.

The learned Nisbet clearly points out, in his valuable work on Scottish Heraldry,—which was another of Sir Hildebrand Osbaldistone's favourite volumes,—that the arms divided by the above partition lines, took their origin simply from the parti-coloured coats which were actually worn as garments when heraldry first arose. The favourite emblematical colours of different princes were thus displayed, in striped or banded patterns, on which symbols were occasionally embroidered or spangled, in gold, silver, or other colours. The custom of wearing heraldic badges embroidered on liveries, was continued in England to a late period, and even till to-day, in the case of the " Beefeaters " ; while livery colours are still retained in use, for men-servants, any heraldic devices being presented only on the coat-buttons.

THE COLOURS OF THE COMMON
CHARGES NOT SYMBOLICAL

THE colours of the common charges were usually
disregarded from a symbolical point of view, unless
there was evidence of a special intent in the colour
of any particular charge. The colours of gutté,
roundles, frets, and roses are, however, exceptions
to the first-named rule. Examples of "counterchanged" arms are very common, and while
these show that the colours of the shield as a
whole were fully regarded, the colours of the
smaller charges were often a matter of indiffer-
ence. The aim of heraldry was to produce the
most striking effect at a glance, and not to dwell
upon the minutiæ of each bearing. Animals were
represented in their natural, or of other colours,
the variations of their colour or of their attitude
being adopted merely as a means of distinction
between one coat and another.

The main colours of the shield and of the
" Honourable Ordinaries" supplied sufficient colour
symbolism, while the particular attributes of the

Ordinaries and common charges added further interesting emblems. The apparent contradictions
sometimes observable in the symbols of one shield
are not more at variance than man's own nature,
which may impel him to war when his heart
inclines to peace, and lead him to hope even amid
afflictions and against desperate odds.

SYMBOLISMS OF THE COMMON CHARGES

IT may be premised that there are several heraldic bearings as to the origin of which nothing definite can be surmised, and to which no symbolism has been ascribed. Some of these are of remote antiquity, and probably originating long before heraldry arose, became assimilated with it by individual assumers of devices. No one has ever pretended that all the bearings to be found in English and foreign heraldry, were originally assumed or conferred as special heraldic emblems. It should be remembered that although the symbols of some particular coat of arms may not denote any particular deed of its first bearer, they may yet express an elevated, animating sentiment, and we may hope that our worthy ancestors "wore the fair flower" of their outward professions as blamelessly as their descendants do in this more enlightened age.

If it should be remarked that I have relied too much upon, and drawn too liberally from, the works of that grand old herald John Guillim, I should reply that I have accepted him as my standard authority, because there is none to equal him among all the old heralds. Guillim published his work shortly after the close of the reign of Elizabeth,—that most interesting period to historians, poets, painters, and novelists,—and he had closely studied all the more ancient writers on the subject, the works of some of whom no longer exist. His honest diligence, learning, and common-sense distinguish him as having been one of the most intelligent men of his time. He was the first to reduce heraldry to a definitive system, or to consult authorities and to attempt to make clear the intentions of English heralds. If it be objected against Guillim's capacity for sound judgment that he inclined to a belief in the powers of witchcraft, it must be remembered that his book was dedicated to the " Modern Solomon," James I., who had himself written a most solemn, and deadly dull, treatise on Demonology. It is a high credential for Guillim that old Sir Hildebrand Osbaldistone used to spend so much time in poring over his and Nisbet's pages, as sweet Diana Vernon affirmed in " Rob Roy."

The LION has always held a high place in heraldry as the emblem of deathless courage. Some of the old heralds give some variations in the meaning of the Lion when borne PASSANT or walking, or if SALIANT or leaping, &c., but as they did not agree as to these definitions, we may now be spared from considering them. There can be no doubt that

| Rampant guardant. | Rampant reguardant. | Passant. | Lion sejant guardant. |

all such differences of attitude were introduced for the sake of variety, and because so many persons were anxious to obtain the lion as an emblem. Guillim, speaking of the lion, says, "It is a lively image of a good soldier, who must be valiant of courage, strong of body, politic in council, and a foe to fear." It is the emblem of St. Mark. In Venice it is borne with wings.

The *Heads of Lions and other Animals* are borne either erased, *i.e.* apparently torn off with jagged pieces at the neck, or *couped, i.e.* cut off cleanly. These severed heads really denote the same as the bearing of the whole animal.

A swan's head gorged with a ducal crown and erased at the neck.

Guillim states that we must interpret all kinds of animals borne in arms or ensigns, in their best sense, according to their most generous and noble qualities, and so therefore to the greatest honour of their bearers. The fox, he says, must not be considered as regards his habits of pilfering and stealing, but as regards his wit and facility of device. An animal may be borne of another colour to its natural state, but if its attitude be *repugnant* to nature, then Guillim holds that it would be disgraceful. It is very unlikely that any one would bear such an ensign, and for this reason I propose to say nothing about those heraldic ",Abatements" which are to be found carefully depicted in all the older works on armory. One cannot imagine any one displaying arms in which appeared the Abatement for "One who had eaten his words," or for "One who had been a traitor to his prince"!

The various nations of Europe have held different standards as to what constituted superiority in heraldic bearings. In the north of Europe the Lion was most esteemed, and especially so in Great Britain, and this animal now occupies three quarterings of our royal arms. In Germany, Austria, and Southern Europe the preference was given to the Eagle, and in France to the Fleur-de-lis, for a similar reason.

The TIGER was held to signify great fierceness and valour when enraged to combat, and symbolises one whose resentment will be dangerous if aroused.

The BEAR was said to possess policy equal to its great strength, and to be the emblem of ferocity in the protection of kindred. It was highly valued as an heraldic device, so that the Baron of Bradwardine was justified in his pride in regard to the "blessed bear," as Scott tells us in "Waverley."

The WOLF is a very ancient and uncommon bearing. It is said by Morgan to denote those valiant captains that do in the end gain their attempts after long sieges and hard enterprises. Guillim speaks of it as being an animal that is wary and careful in attack, and therefore one whom it is dangerous to assail or thwart, since its nature is cruel and relentless. He adds that Macedon, the grandson of Noah, bore this ensign, as also did the Romans. It was also the Egyptian symbol of Anubis the Conductor of the Dead, and the city of Lycopolis derived its name from the veneration in which the wolf was there held. Sir Gardiner Wilkinson states that mummies of wolves have been discovered at O'sioot, on the site of the ancient city of Lycopolis.

WOLF'S HEAD. This was borne by Hugh Lupus,

first Earl of Chester, and nephew of William the Conqueror. He probably derived the cognomen of "Lupus" from this bearing. A wolf's head is borne as the ancient family crest, with two wolves as the armorial supporters, by Viscount Wolseley, now the Commander-in-chief of the British army, whose second title, Baron Cairo, relates to his great military service in the land of Egypt. Few soldiers could show such a record of war around the whole world as the life of this brave strategist presents.

The RHINOCEROS is of immense size and strength, and of great ferocity when aroused. It never seeks combat, but in defence of itself, or its fellows, will fight at all odds. It may be regarded as denoting this character in heraldry, but it is a very rare bearing. It is borne as a crest by the Colvilles, and by the Wades of Essex, and also as a supporter in the arms of Lord Mountcashell.

The ELEPHANT is of huge strength and stature, and very sagacious and courageous. Guillim says it is of "Great strength, greater wit, and greatest ambition." The heraldic signification may be drawn from its courage and strength. The Elephant was the ensign of Cyneus, king of Scythia, and of Idomenes, king of Thessaly. The English Elphinstones bear an elephant in their arms, but the

Scotch family of Elphinstone always displayed three boars' heads, according to Nisbet.

The HERALDIC TIGER is an imaginary beast, which was delighted in by heralds in olden times. It is represented in its body to be similar to a wolf, with a spike on its nose, a knotted mane, and a lion's tail! It is now seldom found in English armory, but it would possess the same signification as that of the ordinary tiger.

The LEOPARD is said to represent a valiant and hardy warrior, who enterprises hazardous things by force and courage. Leopards' heads only are generally found borne in British heraldry, but the animal itself is sometimes borne as a supporter. The lions borne in the English Royal arms are said to have been derived from two leopards borne by Richard I.

A LEOPARD'S HEAD *"jessant"* or *swallowing a fleur-de-lis*. This bearing is said by Newton in his "Display of Heraldry" to have been conferred by Edward III. during his wars in France, as a reward to some of the leaders who served under him in his victorious campaigns—the idea of the device being, that the lion of the English arms is swallowing the lily of the French coat! Fluellen's reference to the swallowing of the leek, in Shakespeare's "Henry V.," occurs to one in connection with this bearing.

E

The PANTHER is rarely found as an heraldic
bearing. It is usually depicted "insensed," a term
applied when flames appear to be issuing from its
mouth and ears. Guillim says, "As a lion may be
said to signify a brave man, so may a panther a
beautiful woman, which, though fierce, is very
tender and loving to her young, and will defend
it with the hazard of her life."

The HORSE. "Of all beasts the most noble and
most useful to man, either in peace or war." It
signifies readiness for all employments for king
and country, and is one of the principal bearings
in armory. A white horse was the ensign of the
Saxons when first they invaded England, and this
bearing is still to be found in memory of our Saxon
ancestors in the arms of Hanover.

> "A steede, a steede of matchless speede,
>   A sword of metal keene,
> All else to noble minds is dross,
>   All else on earth is meane.
> And O the thundering press of knights
>   When loud their war-cries swell,
> Might serve to call a saint from heaven,
>   Or rouse a fiend from hell!"

The MULE. This bearing, Guillim says, may well
be borne by abbots and abbesses, who bear the
mitre and cross, which are the emblems of pastoral

jurisdiction, but have not the actual exercise of such.

The Ass is the emblem of patience and humility. The arms of the Askew family, of which Anne Askew, the gentle martyr, was a member, were, on a white or silver shield a Fess, between three asses passant, or walking, all of sable or black.

The BULL or OX. Guillim says, " The bearing of a bull or the head thereof is a note of valour and magnanimity." An ox was borne by the Athenians on one of their coins, and it was also worshipped as a god by the Egyptians, under the name of Apis, "the soul of Osiris." A specially marked living bull was always kept as the object of this worship.

The BOAR, Guillim says, " is a fierce combatant when at bay, and ceases fighting only with its life, and therefore may be properly applied as the armorial bearing of a warrior." A white boar was the badge of Richard III.

BOAR'S HEAD. I have referred to this on page 31. It was accepted as an emblem of hospitality, besides being, as I have stated, a most important feudal offering.

The GOAT. Guillim says that this animal is the emblem of that martial man who wins a victory by the employment rather of policy than valour. " It may betoken one that is willing to fare hard, so he may be in high employment honoured." (Sloane Evans.*)

The LAMB is symbolical of gentleness and patience under suffering. This is certainly often borne with a scriptural allusion in view.

The HOLY LAMB or AGNUS DEI. A lamb depicted carrying either a crossed staff or a banner of the cross of St. George, and with glory above its head. This is the emblem of faith, being typical of the gentle-natured founder of the Christian Church. This kind of bearing, Guillim says, " may well befit a brave, resolute spirit who undertakes a war in Christ's cause." It is the ensign of the Middle Temple, and was also borne in the arms of Gothland, and is found in various English arms. (See page 152.)

The RAM is the Duke or leader of the flock, and signifies authority. Sloane Evans mentions that it was highly esteemed by the Thebans. Count D'Alviella states that the ram was one of the Egyptian symbols for the sun. Its signification in heraldry would be "a leader."

LAMB'S FLEECE. This is appropriately borne by the Jason family. The knightly order of the Fleece of Gold indicates the ancient honour of this symbol, and it is proved by Miss Ellen Millington in her interesting work on Heraldry (London, 1858),

* "A Grammar of British Heraldry," by Rev. W. Sloane Evans, B.A. London : J. Russell Smith, 1854.

that in founding this order special reference was made to the fleece of Gideon.

HARES and RABBITS (the latter are heraldically termed *Conies*). These animals were probably introduced into heraldry to betoken one who enjoys a peaceable and retired life. It is also quite likely that a scriptural reference to conies was intended.

The SQUIRREL. A lover of the woods, and therefore emblematical of sylvan retirement being the delight of its bearer.

HEDGEHOG. Sloane Evans says that the signification of this bearing is a "Provident provider." It is borne by the Harris family, and also by the family of Herries of Scotland.

The BEAVER. Denotes industry and perseverance, and is borne in the arms of Canada.

The FOX. The application of this symbol in heraldry denotes one who will use all that he may possess of sagacity, wit, or wisdom in his own defence. (See page 62.)

The TALBOT, MASTIFF, and GREYHOUND. It has been observed that there is scarcely any virtue possessed by man that is not shared by the various kinds of dogs. The signification of either of these

Greyhound.

would be courage, vigilancy, and loyal fidelity. A

talbot is the only device within the shield of the ancient family of Wolseley of Staffordshire, whose crest of a wolf's head has been previously referred to.

The CAT, or CAT-A-MOUNTAIN. Sloane Evans says this was once the emblem of the Dutch nation, and signifies liberty, vigilance, forecast, and courage. Among the Egyptians the cat was held sacred to the goddess Pasht or Bubastis, *i.e.* Diana the huntress.

The CAMEL. Sloane Evans gives the symbolism of this bearing as being "docility, patience, and indefatigable perseverance."

The BEE was reckoned by the Egyptians as an emblem of regal power. In armory it is used to represent well-governed industry. Bees were adopted by Napoleon I. in his arms, and have since been used by his family. They are also found borne in British heraldry.

The ANT, Guillim says, "may signify a man of great labour, wisdom, and providence in all his affairs." It has been occasionally borne in armory.

The SPIDER. This insect, Guillim says, may signify wisdom, labour, and prudence. I do not remember having met with any instance of its having been borne in English arms.

The GRASSHOPPER, among the Athenians, was held as "a special emblem of nobility, and therefore they used to wear golden grasshoppers in their hair, to signify that they were descended from a noble race, and home-bred, for where this insect is bred, there it will live and die." Solomon reckoned it as "One of the four small things in the earth that are full of wisdom." (Guillim.) Sir Thomas Gresham, who founded the Royal Exchange in the time of Elizabeth, set this, his armorial cognisance, at the top of that building.

The HOUSE SNAIL. Although this little creature moves slowly, it can by perseverance ascend to the highest places, where even the lion cannot go. It is an emblem of deliberation and perseverance. (Guillim.) It has been borne in English heraldry by one of the families of Shelly, and, according to Nisbet, by the families of Barton and Studman.

The DOUBLE EAGLE. Borne in the arms of Russia and Austria. In that recent very interesting and most valuable work, "The Migration of Symbols,"* by Count Goblet d'Alviella, it is pointed out that the first example of this emblem is found in a bas-relief at Eyak, which dates back to the civilisation of the Hittites. Count D'Alviella considers that this figure was first introduced into Europe at the time of the Crusades, and it would appear that there is an entire absence of proof of

---

* With an introduction by Sir George Birdwood, M.D., K.C.I.E. Westminster: Constable & Co., 1894.

any example of this singular bearing being used in Europe at an earlier period.

The EAGLE, which is usually represented with

An eagle argent
displayed.

wings "displayed," signifies "a man of action, ever more occupied in high and weighty affairs, and one of lofty spirit, ingenious, speedy in apprehension, and judicious in matters of ambiguity." The displayed wings signify protection, and the gripping talons "rending and ruin to rebels and evil-doers." (Guillim.) The Eagle was an ensign of the ancient kings of Persia and Babylon; and Marius, 102 B.C., made the Eagle alone the ensign at the head of the Roman legions, but previous to this they had borne the Minotaur, horse, wolf, and boar. The emperors of the Western Roman Empire used a

An eagle sable,
displayed, within a
bordure engrailed.

black eagle, but those of the Eastern or Byzantine Roman Empire adopted a golden one. Since the Romans, many empires and kingdoms have taken the eagle for their ensign, viz., Austria, Prussia, Russia, Poland, France, and also, as a supporter and crest, the Republic of America. The two-headed eagle signifies a double empire. William Rufus adopted as a device an eagle looking towards the sun, with the motto "Preferro," or "I can endure it." (Timbs.) Sloane Evans remarks that the Egyptians paid the Eagle high honours at Heliopolis. I think he meant the vulture or hawk, which was sacred to their highest god, Ra, or the Sun god. The Eagle is also held to be typical of a noble nature from its strength and innate power, and has been very generally preferred in Continental heraldry as a high device. Guillim says that true magnanimity and fortitude of mind is signified by the Eagle, which disdains to combat with smaller birds. The Scriptures make constant reference to the Eagle as a symbol of power. It is also the emblem of St. John the Evangelist.

ALERION. This is an eagle "displayed," but without beak or claws. The origin of this bearing is a matter of doubt. Nisbet says it might refer to one who having been maimed and lamed in war, was thus prevented from fully asserting his power.

WINGS are hieroglyphics of celerity and sometimes of protection or coverture. (Guillim.) When wings are borne they are supposed to

Wings conjoined "in lure."

pertain to the eagle, unless otherwise described. A pair of wings is termed *conjoined*, and is shown either with the tips of the wings turned upwards, called "elevated," or turned downwards, called "inverted," or "in lure," as in the arms of Seymour or St. Maur, Duke of Somerset.

The LEG or CLAW OF A BIRD is always taken to be that of an eagle, unless otherwise expressed. It seems to say, "Behold the preyer upon others has been preyed upon." If the bird be not one of prey, this symbolism would be changed accordingly. Griffins' legs and those of animals of prey are also occasionally borne in arms, and possess the same signification as that given to the eagle's claw.

FEATHERS. Those used in heraldry are usually of the Ostrich, and signify willing obedience and serenity. Guillim recites that King Stephen bore a plume of feathers with the motto "No force alters their fashion," referring to the fold or fall of the feather recovering itself after being ruffled by the wind. When a feather is borne with its quill trans-

fixing a scroll of parchment, it is called an escrol. The latter was borne as a device by Roger Clarendon, natural son of the Black Prince.

The PLUME OF FEATHERS borne as the crest of the Prince of Wales would signify "willing obedience and serenity of mind." The legend as to this crest having been captured in war by the Black Prince lacks support, and is far less likely than that he adopted it as a crest because so many of his family and predecessors bore either one or two feathers as a badge or cognisance. The original bearing of feathers in heraldry is said to have been derived from the Crusades, but it is highly probable that these and a great many other ancient Eastern symbols, subsequently used in heraldry, were at an early period derived in Western Europe from Egypt, either through the Romans, or later through the Gnostics of the second or third centuries. I have elsewhere remarked, that to biblical references and to associations connected with religion belong a very large number of the emblems found in arms. If one considers the influence of religious sentiment in Europe at the time when heraldry flourished, this conviction is sustained, and one is quite justified in seeking for Scriptural passages in explanation of any ancient coat of arms, in which symbols appear that are capable of being interpreted by such reference. For centuries after the introduction of crests, feathers were often preferred for the decoration of the helmet, and are still retained in military wear in the hats of generals and staff officers.

The FALCON or HAWK was an Egyptian hieroglyphic of the Sun god. In heraldry it signifies

one eager or hot in the pursuit of an object much
desired. (Sloane Evans.) It is represented either
close, rising, or volant, *i.e.* flying. Guillim says of
the bearing of a hawk seated on its "rest," it may
signify a bearer who is ready and serviceable for
high affairs, though he lives at rest and unemployed.
The latter bearing is found in the arms of the
Hawkers, now represented by Col. W. S. Hawker,
D.L., of Cornwall. As to the bearing of *Hawks'
or Falcons' lures*, these are supposed to typify one
who was fond of the highest pursuits, such as
hunting and falconry were considered to be in the
palmy days of heraldry. The "lure" was constructed of a pair of wings, so fashioned as to
resemble a bird, and which was thrown up to call
back the falcon when it had flown too far afield
after the quarry. It would therefore be "a signal
to recall the absent from afar." It is borne on a
bend by the Wades of Cornwall, and by some other
branches of that family.

HAWKS' or FALCONS' BELLS. (See page 147.)

The KITE was held in honour among the
Egyptians in their auguries and predictions. I
do not remember any instance of its being borne
in English arms.

The PARROT is found in several British arms, and
was also frequently borne by Swiss families. I have
met with no symbolism for this bearing.

The OWL. The Egyptian hieroglyphic of death. It betokens in arms one who is vigilant and of acute wit. It was the favourite bird of Minerva, and was borne by the Athenians in their standards. Guillim says it intimates that the true and vigilant man never sleeps. It is frequently found in English arms.

The PEACOCK is the most beautiful and proudest of birds, and might perchance have been first used in heraldry on account of its beauty and pride of carriage. It is the bird of "Juno, Queen of Heaven," and might perhaps have been borne on shield or helm at the tourney or joust, by some favoured knight in reference to his "fair lady Dulcinea of Toboso," whose beauty, he considered, overshadowed that of other dames. It was believed by the ancient races that the peacock was a destroyer of serpents. There are many examples of its use in English heraldry, and English knights would sometimes swear "by the peacock." It also formed one of the principal dishes at State banquets.

The PELICAN feeding her young adorned the altars of many of the temples of the Egyptians, and was emblematical of the duties of a parent. She is represented either "vulning" or wounding her breast with her beak ; or, "in her Piety," when surrounded by her young who are being fed by the parent. This symbol has often been used by the Church as the emblem of devoted and self-sacrificing charity, with the motto "Sic Christus dilexit nos." The pelican is the device of the Inner Temple, London.

The STORK, Guillim states, is the emblem of filial duty, inasmuch as it renders obedience and nourishment to its parents, and it is also the emblem of a grateful man. Sloane Evans mentions that the ancients paid divine honours to this bird. In Egypt the Ibis was sacred to the god Thoth. I think that heraldry has taken the Stork and Heron in the place of the extinct Ibis, which was a similar but smaller bird.

The SWAN, Apollo's bird. The ensign of the poets, and the hieroglyphic of a musical person, because of its anciently supposed habit of singing sweetly in the hour of death. Its heraldic meaning would stand for "a lover of poetry and harmony," or, as Nisbet says, for a learned person.

The CYGNET is a young swan. If represented with a ducal coronet around its neck, from which a chain is reflected

Cygnet Royal.

over its back, it is called a Cygnet Royal. I have referred on page 116 to the bearing of chains on animals. The Swan's head and neck, gorged with a crown around the latter, is a bearing of high dignity, and has the same signification as the swan itself, and the same may be said respecting the bearing of the heads of other birds and animals. (See page 61.)

The GOOSE and DUCK. Guillim says, by flying, running, and swimming under water, these birds have many ways of eluding their enemies and beguiling their hopes. They may therefore be held to signify a man of many resources.

The GANNET is a duck represented without feet or legs, and the ancient heralds may have intended this to represent the same meaning which Guillim gave to the footless swallow or *Martlet*, viz., that it represented one who had to "subsist by the *wings* of his virtue and merit, having little land to rest upon." For this reason he says the *Martlet* is the "difference" given on the shield of a younger brother. Some have supposed that the *Martlet* derived its footless representation in heraldry from the appearance of the bird of Paradise to ancient Eastern travellers.

The SWALLOW is the harbinger of Spring. "It is a good bearing for one who is prompt and ready in the despatch of his business," says Guillim. It

is also an emblem for the bringer of good news.
Lord Arundell of Wardour bears six "hirundells,"
or swallows. This coat is one of the most ancient
in Cornwall, Lord Arundell being the lineal descendant of the Cornish Arundells.

The COCK is a bird of great courage, always
prepared for battle, and it frequently fights to the
death. Being the herald of dawn, it is often used
as an emblem of watchfulness, and may be used
in armory to signify either a hero in the field or an
able man in the senate. (Guillim.) It was used in
ancient times in Asia Minor as a symbol of the
sun. (D'Alviella's " Migration of Symbols.")

The DOVE is a symbol of the Holy Spirit in the
Church, and it represents in armory "loving
constancy and peace." It was an ensign of the
Syrians. When represented with an olive branch
in its bill, it is intended to symbolise a harbinger
of good tidings, in reference to the dove which
returned to Noah. It is found as a symbol of
worship, on a jewel discovered at Mycenæ by Dr.
Schliemann. Doves or pigeons have often proved
most useful messengers.

The RAVEN was esteemed as a symbol by the
Romans, and it was an ensign of the Danes when
they invaded England in circa A.D. 870. The Rev.
W. Sloane Evans holds, in his interesting work on

heraldry, that this bird is emblematical of him who, having derived little from his ancestors, has through Providence become the architect of his own fortunes ; but I have elsewhere met with the definition of it as representing one of an enduring constancy of nature, and I think the latter is the probable anciently accepted symbolism. Evans's definition would be inappropriate for an *hereditary* cognisance. The Danes regarded the Raven as being consecrated to Wodin, their God of War, and they held that it possessed necromantic powers as an augur, in determining by its attitudes in flight whether any expedition would be successful or otherwise.

The CROW. Mr. Sloane Evans gives this as the emblem of "long life," but why any one should venture to predict long life for himself, it is difficult to understand. I suggest "a settled habitation and a quiet life" as being the more probable signification in connection with this bearing. One is reminded here of Tennyson's amusing mistake when he wrote in "Locksley Hall" of

"A many winter'd crow,
That leads the clanging rookery home."

Of course no rooks would accept the leadership of a crow, nor would this solitary bird accept of such

F

a situation. However, for heraldic purposes we may be allowed to confound the crows with the rooks, as they are so much alike at a distance.

The Cornish Chough is called "the king of crows." "A noble bearing of great antiquity, and may betoken the bearer thereof to be a man of stratagems to the disadvantage of his enemies." This definition is not in direct contradiction to Guillim's other statement, that the Chough might betoken "watchful activity for friends," as the two qualifications might well be combined. Cardinal Wolsey bore Cornish Choughs. This bird has a red beak and legs in the English variety, which differs from the Austrian Carinthian Chough, the legs and beak of which are yellow. The Cornish variety of late years has become very scarce.

FISHES are not, says Guillim, of so high a nature as a bearing in coat armour when considered by themselves, but being borne by many persons of royal or noble families, are so ennobled that they are to be preferred before many that are formed of beasts or birds. On the subject of the comparative value of various bearings in armory he observes, " Forasmuch as the living things before named have their virtues worthy imitation, that it is a chief glory to gentlemen of coat armour to have their virtues displayed under the types and forms of such things as they bear, it is to be wished that each one of them would considerately examine the commendable properties of such significant tokens as they do bear, and do his best to manifest to the world that he hath the like in himself; for it is rather a dishonour than a praise for a man to bear a lion on his shield, if he bear a sheep in his heart or a goose in his brain, being therein like those ships which bear the names of "Victory," "Dreadnought," and the like, though sometimes it speed with them contrary to their titles. A true, generous mind will endeavour that for his self virtues he may be esteemed, and not insist only upon the fame and merit of his progenitors, the praise whereof belongs to them and not to him." And he further remarks elsewhere, "This, therefore, must be recommended for a general rule, that the worthiness of the bearer is not the least respect we should use in considering the dignity of things borne in coat armour."

Dolphin.

The DOLPHIN was said to be an affectionate fish, and fond of music. It was the crest of the "Dauphin," or heir to the throne of France, who is said to have taken this title from his cognisance. Guillim says, "In this fish is proposed to us an example of charity and kind affection towards our children."

The LUCE or PIKE is frequently borne in arms, but I have not found any particular heraldic signification applied to it. This is very probably one of the symbols borrowed from the early Christian

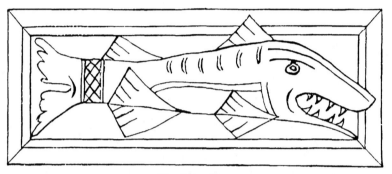

Heraldic pike.

Church, in which a fish was used as one of the symbols of Christ, and fish are often found borne in threes in reference to the Trinity. A good deal of interesting information is obtainable on this subject in Moule's " Heraldry of Fish."

The TORTOISE signifies invulnerability to attack, according to Washbourne's " Heraldry of Crests." Nisbet states that the family of Gowdie, in England, bore on a blue shield a tortoise of gold. Instances are obtainable of the bearing of crabs, lobsters, and of fishing nets, hooks, and baskets. The particular meanings of these have not been defined by any writer, and such bearings may be generally applicable, like hunting gear, to indicate lovers of such forms of useful employment.

The UNICORN is one of the heraldic fabulous beasts. I have mentioned elsewhere that some writers believed the rhinoceros was changed by tradition into this horned horse, while· others have thought that the narwhale gave rise to the idea. The old writers relate that the Unicorn was famous for its virtue, courage, and strength, and that its horn was supposed to be the most powerful antidote against poisons. It is much used in heraldry, and signifies extreme courage. It is borne in the arms of Ker, as well as by many other families.

The GRIFFIN. This chimerical creature has the head, wings, and talons of an eagle, and the body of a lion. It is one of the principal bearings in heraldry, but chiefly as a crest or supporter. Guillim says that it " sets forth the property of a valorous soldier whose magnanimity is such that he will dare all dangers, and even death itself, rather than become captive." It also symbolised Vigilancy, and is found to be as old as the time of the Phœnicians, as shown by Count D'Alviella.

Griffin.

The DRAGON. Our poets feign that Dragons sit brooding on riches and treasures, which are committed to their charge because of their admirable

Dragon.

sharpness of sight, and that they are supposed of all other living creatures to be the most valiant. (Guillim.) It therefore stands as the symbol of a most valiant defender of treasure. Hovedon tells us that Cuthred, king of Wessex, bore a gold dragon at the battle of Bureford. King Arthur, it is stated, bore a red dragon. This beast is always represented as being encased in stout scales resembling armour. The Tudor sovereigns bore a red dragon as a cognisance, but Queen Elizabeth changed the colour to gold.

The heads of the griffin and the dragon are very frequently used in armory, generally as crests, and each would signify the same as the bearing of the entire body of one of these grim monsters.

The WYVERN is a dragon, represented with two

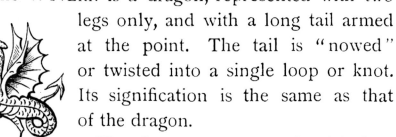

Cockatrice.

legs only, and with a long tail armed at the point. The tail is "nowed" or twisted into a single loop or knot. Its signification is the same as that of the dragon.

The COCKATRICE was the fabulous king of serpents, although some held that it was only a foot long. It was supposed that its breath and sight were so poisonous and deadly as to kill all who came within their range. It was the emblem of "terror to all beholders." The *Basilisk* is a similar device.

The SPHINX. An ancient statue highly esteemed by the Egyptians, having the face and breast of a woman, and the body of a lion. It was supposed to represent omniscience and secrecy. It is borne by the English regiments which were engaged at the battle of Alexandria under Abercromby. The Thebans bore a Sphinx in memory of the monster overcome by Ædipus.

The SALAMANDER is an animal resembling a small dragon, and represented as living in flames of fire. It is very rarely borne in British heraldry; but Nisbet gives an example of its bearing by one of the branches of the Douglas family. Mr. Andrew Lang states that a Salamander was used as a device by Francis I. of France. I have recently met with one borne, on a book-plate, as the crest of the family of Smiith.

The PEGASUS. Typified "exceeding activity and energy of mind whereby one may mount to honour." (Guillim.) Nisbet presents it in the arms of M'Quin, Scotland. It is well known as an emblem of poetic genius or inspiration.

The HARPY is represented with a virgin's face,

neck, and breast, with the body of a lion, and wings and talons of an eagle. It signified Ferocity under provocation.

The MERMAID exhibits the face, neck, and breast of a woman, and the body and tail of a fish. It is usually represented with dishevelled hair and holding a mirror. It was used as a symbol of eloquence. (Sloane Evans.)

The CENTAUR. This, like many other heraldic figures, was taken from the ancient classics, or more remotely still from ancient Egypt, as it is one of the Egyptian signs of the zodiac.* Old writers state that the first warrior seen on horseback was taken to be half man and half beast, and so terrified the enemy that they took flight. It is said to have been borne as a device by King Stephen in 1135, in consequence of his having entered England and obtained the victory when the sun was in that sign. This legend is doubted by Planché. Its use in arms is supposed to be applicable to those who have been eminent in the field.

HYDRA. A dragon with seven heads. It is seldom or never found in heraldry, but would signify the conquest of a very powerful enemy. In this sense it is employed to decorate the hilt of

* D'Alviella speaks of the fantastic fauna of the East having formed the symbolic menagery of the West, in the Middle Ages.

a particularly handsome presentation sword of honour bestowed in 1807 on Captain William Rogers, R.N., who with most conspicuous gallantry captured a large French privateer of seven guns, when he was in command of the Royal packet brig *Windsor Castle* of only one gun. This sword is now in my collection.

The PHŒNIX. This bird was represented to be as large as the eagle. It was held that only one existed at the same time, and which, according to the ancient writers, lived 500 years, and when her end approached she made her nest, which latter, igniting by the heat of the sun, destroyed her, but out of her ashes arose another phœnix. It was often used of old as an emblem of the Resurrection, sometimes with the motto "Resurgam." It is often used in heraldry.

STAG, HART, BUCK, and DEER. According to Guillim and Upton, these animals are symbolical either of one skilful in music and a lover of harmony, or of one that is politic and well foresees his times and opportunities; or again, of one who is unwilling to assail the enemy rashly, but rather desirous to stand on his own ground honestly than to annoy another wrongfully. These definitions may be summarised

Stag.

briefly to signify Policy, Peace, and Harmony. See page 30.

HINDS and DOES are seldom used in heraldry, as, being unarmed with horns or antlers, they are, according to Guillim, considered of less worth as a bearing.

HORNS and ANTLERS. The same authority states that these denote in arms, strength and fortitude. They are much used in heraldry, and especially so throughout Germany. A Scriptural reference is, I think, manifested in their being so extensively used in armory. "The horns of the righteous shall be exalted," may well have been the mediæval intent

Two bucks courant.

in bearing such symbols. Count D'Alviella, in his "Migration of Symbols," points out that horns were used as symbols of the Divine power in Assyria, Mesopotamia, and Egypt from the earliest times. There can be no doubt that many of such emblems have found their way into British and Continental heraldry from the remotest times, having been handed down as talismans from antiquity by family and tribal traditions. Although their original symbolisms had been completely forgotten, they were still proudly borne in arms, and new meanings, derived from scriptural or other sources, were attributed to them.

The ESCALLOP SHELL attached to the hood or hat was the pilgrim's emblem in his expeditions to holy places, and became such a distinguished ensign that Pope Alexander the Fourth allowed it to none but pilgrims who were truly noble. It was afterwards introduced into armory as signifying one who had made long journeys or voyages to far countries, who had borne considerable naval command, or who had gained great victories. (Washbourne's "Heraldry of Crests.") Guillim speaks of its signification in the latter terms only, but it is borne for either symbolism, and especially for a successful commander. It was the emblem of Santiago or St. James, and is of frequent occurrence in arms.

OTHER SHELLS, Guillim says, may be regarded as signifying the goodness and wisdom of God to His creatures, in protecting them against dangers, or in other words, they signify the Protection of Providence.

The HEART, Guillim remarks, was regarded by the ancients as signifying a man of sincerity, and such a one as speaks the truth from his heart. It is sometimes used in heraldry in this sense, but more often as the emblem of Charity.

FLAMING HEART. This, says Morgan, is a type of ardent affection. The families of Wade of Durham, Ireland, and Canada, bear a shield divided *per* Fess wavy, gold and green, in the chief or top part, a human heart emitting flames of fire in proper colours, between two cross crosslets of black, and in the lower part of the shield is an anchor erect of the last colour. Crest, a dove and branch, all "proper" and charged with a crosslet. I have noticed this bearing fully, because it is so very symbolical, and it is by no means of modern composition. It was confirmed, as an ancient bearing, in 1768 by Heralds' College.

The HAND is the pledge of Faith, sincerity, and justice. *Two right hands conjoined* denote Union and alliance.

The hand is found as a symbol on a Chaldæan cylinder, as well as at Carthage. (D'Alviella.)

A red hand is the usual mark for a baronet if borne on a small inescutcheon.

The ARM signifies a laborious and industrious person. The three arms conjoined, with fists clenched, borne by the Tremaynes, now represented by John Tremayne, Esq., D.L., of Sydenham,

Devon, and of Heligan, Cornwall, may signify a triple offer of revenge for an injury done to the name or fame of the first bearer. (Guillim.) An arm encased in armour denotes one fitted for the performance of high enterprises. (Guillim.)

GAUNTLETS also signify a man armed for the performance of martial enterprise.

The LEG is emblematical of strength, stability, and expedition, especially of the latter, and Guillim assigns the same meaning to the bearing of a Shoe or Foot.

The HUMAN HEAD stands for honour. The heads of "blackamoors" or negroes generally refer to deeds of prowess in the Crusades. See the remarks on page 144 concerning the human figure.

SKULLS and *crossed thigh-bones*, the well-known emblems of mortality, occasionally are found borne in heraldry. The skull was an emblem borne by the Thracians.

The EYE signifies Providence in Government. Queen Elizabeth is represented in Lodge's Portraits, wearing a dress on which human eyes and ears are embroidered, and on the sleeve of which is a large snake. These were all intended as symbolical devices.

MILLSTONES. Guillim thinks these may signify "the mutual converse of human society," since they are never used singly, but in couples, each standing in need of the other's aid for the performance of its work. The Cross Moline is supposed to represent a mill-rind, and is often called the Miller's Cross or a "Cross Miller."

SCEPTRE. The emblem of Justice. (Guillim.)

TRIDENT. The symbol of Maritime dominion.

CROWN. Royal or seigniorial authority ; or if a celestial crown is intended, the reference would be to a heavenly reward. (Guillim.)

PASTORAL CROSIER. The emblem of a shepherd's watchfulness over his flock, and denotes episcopal jurisdiction and authority. (Guillim.) Two Crosiers are borne by the family of Lammie of Scotland.

Crosier, bearing a cross, lamb, and lily as sacred emblems.

The FINGER RING or the ANNULET is well known

as the emblem of fidelity. Joseph was highly honoured by the one given to him by Pharaoh. The Romans are said to have worn a ring as a sign of knighthood, and one is still used at coronations and in some institutions of knighthood.

Annulets.

The LOZENGE, like all other square figures, represents honesty and constancy, and it was also held to be a token of noble birth The ancient family of Feilden (or, as one branch spells the name, Feilding) bears three lozenges on a Fess. Our plate gives a lozenge-shaped shield, on which a lady's arms are always borne if she be either unmarried or a widow.

Lozenge-shaped shield, bearing an engrailed pale.

BILLETS. These oblong figures, Guillim states, are representative of letters folded for transmission. He quotes an ancient heraldic manuscript, which defines their signification in the following words: "That their first bearer was a man who obtained credence, knowledge, and faith in his words and deeds, and who was

A billet argent on a shield azure.

secret in his affairs." Nisbet offers an example of this symbolism in the family of Callendar, who acted as clerks for the early Scotch kings, and were the only ancient Scottish family which bore billets.

TEXT LETTERS are sometimes borne on shields, and I think these may stand for the initials of great battles or tournaments, such as Ascalon, Tournay, or Ashby-de-la-Zouche in the case of the letter Z. Modern heralds have sometimes inscribed the whole name of a battle on the escutcheon of arms.

The PEN, Guillim remarks, is the emblem of the liberal art of writing and of learned employments. He quotes a curious old couplet which refers to the power of parchment, pen, and wax in binding all men in the affairs of life :

> "The calf, the goose, the bee,
> The world is ruled by these three."

He says that the INKHORN would bear the same signification as that of the pen. Both have been borne in armory.

The HARP and LYRE. Guillim states the harp was anciently used to signify "one who was of a well-composed and tempered judgment." It is held to mean "Contemplation" when referred to as a poetic symbol, and would have the same meaning in armory. We have various Scriptural references to this instrument, such as

> "I will open my dark saying upon the harp."—*Psalm* xlix.
> "We hanged our harps upon the willows."—*Psalm* cxxxvii.

Tennyson's lines might also here be fittingly recalled :

> "And love took up the harp of life,
> And smote on all the chords with might."

A harp is borne by the Everest family; and

Papworth gives an ancient coat of Fogarty, viz., on a silver shield a "jews'-harp" lying bendwise between six laurel leaves. This was really a lyre, which possesses the same symbolism. Guillim gives the arms of Frances: An Ermine shield with a black Canton, on which is a silver harp. The harp is also the Irish heraldic symbol, now borne in the third quartering of the Royal arms of England.

AGRICULTURAL IMPLEMENTS. Guillim, speaking of these, says, "Agricultural pursuits have always been reckoned in high esteem by all nations, and such implements as are used in husbandry. The artificial and mechanical sciences or professions are as necessary for man's use and support and traffic of society, as the liberal arts and sciences. These (Agricultural Implements), therefore, are not to be condemned, since they are the express image of trades very behoveful to man, and their exquisite skill issued out of the plentiful fountain of God's abundant spirit. No special signification has been attributed to the bearing of the Harrow, Plough, &c., but the remarks quoted above of our old heraldic philosopher would give to each of these agricultural bearings the meaning of "labouring in the earth and depending upon Providence for the event."

G

The *Scythe* and *Sickle* express the hope of a fruitful harvest of things hoped for.

LEVELS and PLUMMETS. Guillim says of these, that they are "the type of equity and uprightness in all our actions, which are to be rectified by the rule of reason and justice; for the plummet ever falls right howsoever it be held, and whatever betide a virtuous man, his actions and conscience will be incorrupt and uncontrollable."

CARPENTERS' SQUARES, he says, "are used by workmen, that in all their works there shall nothing be found done either rashly or by adventure, and which teach that men should use the some moderation in the performance of those actions of virtue wherein man's happiness consists." These, then, denote as a symbol, that the bearer would desire to conform all his actions to the laws of right and equity.

HAMMER. He says, "This is an honourable emblem, and may be borne crowned, as in the arms of the ancient London Company of Smiths, inasmuch as the use of iron is more precious and necessary for a commonwealth than gold is, for which reason the Philistines would not allow a smith to dwell among the Israelites, lest they should make them swords and spears." The *hammer, anvil,* and *pincers* are the chief emblems of the smith's trade. The Martel was a military hammer used in conflict. The double - headed Hammer was the chief emblem of Thor.

The ANCHOR signifies succour in extremity, and is also the Christian emblem of hope, in which latter sense it is usually borne in armory. Cosmo de' Medici, Duke of Etruria, bore as a device two anchors, with the motto " Duabus," meaning, it was good to have two holdfasts to trust to. Richard I. once bore as a device one anchor, with the motto " Christus Duce." Other bearings relating to ships, such as rudders, masts, sails, boats, &c., are borne in arms, especially in foreign heraldry. I have not found any symbolisms assigned to these bearings, but there can be little doubt that they were adopted with the intent of commemorating some special action performed, or danger escaped, in connection with the " world of waters."

SHIP, LYMPHIAD, or GALLEY. Such bearings are often met with in British heraldry, and the remarks in the preceding paragraph are also applicable to these. All such symbols would point to some notable expedition by sea, by which perhaps the first bearers had become famous. In the case of the more ancient bearing of all these kinds of simple emblems by old families, they may have been derived by tradition from the earliest times, long anterior to any written records of such families, or to the wearing of coats of arms.

CUBES, SQUARES, or DICE. Guillim says of these bearings, that as they fall right however they be cast, they are emblems of constancy, but he adds, "Dicers who trust their fortunes to them find it otherwise." He says elsewhere that *all square figures*, such as lozenges, signify Constancy. *Chequy, Lozengy, Gobbonny*, and *Compony* are therefore to be classed under the same signification. Morgan in his "Sphere of Gentry" says, "Square figures are symbols of Wisdom, and signify Verity, probity, constancy, and equity. The phrase as to "square dealings" perhaps arose from such symbols, which are of high consideration among Freemasons.

The AXE is the symbol of the execution of military duty, and is also referred to symbolically in the Scriptures.

The PURSE, Guillim ascribes to be the emblem of a frank and liberal steward of the blessings that God has bestowed upon him. It is the official emblem of a treasurer.

A TOWER or CASTLE is the emblem of grandeur and solidity, and has been granted sometimes to one who has faithfully held one for his king, or who has captured one by force or stratagem. There may also be a scriptural reference intended.

BRIDGE. This, according to Guillim, may signify the cares and patient stability of men in magis-
tracy, who must endure the assaults, taunts, and
envy of the discontented and vulgar. It may therefore be said to signify a governor or magistrate.

The PILLAR or COLUMN signifies, says Guillim,
Fortitude and Constancy. · A serpent coiled round
a column would mean wisdom with fortitude. A
shattered column is the sepulchral emblem erected
over the grave of the head of a family.

The SNAKE is the emblem of Wisdom. The
Egyptians represented the world by the figure of a
serpent biting its tail. The brazen serpent erected
by Moses, proves the remote antiquity of the snake
as a symbol.

A SCALING-LADDER denotes one who was fearless
in attacking, as such is used in warfare only by extremely brave soldiers. Where it is represented placed
against a tower, Guillim says it " may put us in mind
to stand carefully on our guard who live in this world,
as in a castle continually assailed by our
spiritual and corporal enemies." Castles and
towers are often borne in English heraldry.

CROSSES. These are borne as charges
in an infinite variety of forms, an excellent enumeration of which is to be
found in Mr. C. N. Elvin's "Dictionary of Heraldry,"

Cross bottonée,
fitchée or
sharpened at
the end.

published in 1889. This work and those by Messrs.
Cussans, Worthy, and Boutell, the latter re-edited by
Mr. Aveling, are full of information regarding the
technicalities of the Science of Arms. The special

Maltese
cross.

German cross.

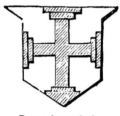

Cross degraded or
with steps.

meaning to be attached to some of the various kinds
of crosses can scarcely be determined unless one
knows the history of each first assumer. That the
Cross in almost every instance had reference to
some Christian experience or sentiment, cannot be

Cross triparted.

Cross avellane.

Cross moline, or
Miller's cross.

doubted. On this subject I have previously made
several remarks while speaking of the larger crosses
which are used as "Ordinaries." Speaking of the
Cross Potent, Guillim says, this is formed as the

handle of a crutch or support for the aged and feeble, and might therefore indicate one whose support is the Cross. Of the Cross on three degrees or steps, called the Cross of Calvary, he says, that the three steps signify the approach thereto, being by Faith, Hope, and Charity. The Cross Crosslet being crossed at each of the four points, is said to signify "the fourfold mystery of

Cross bottonée or treflée.

Cross patoncée, voided or outlined in black.

Dismembered cross.

the Cross." The red cross of the mediæval Rosicrucians, or Brethren of the Rosy Cross, has been fully described in Hargreave Jennings's valuable symbolical work on the Rosicrucians. (See the Cross as an "Ordinary," on page 43.) Saltires are sometimes found borne as charges instead of as Ordinaries, that is, if two or more occur in the same arms.

Trestles and Stools. Guillim says these may be taken as a special note of hospitality. He gives an illustration of the arms of a family named Stratford, who bore a table between three trestles or stools. I may mention that the table bore nothing upon it. Guillim states that the bearing sometimes called a "fess humée" is really a table and not a fess. See plate on next page.

CUSHIONS. F. Nichols states that these have been looked upon as marks of authority, and have been borne by several noble families.

ANGELS, CHERUBS, and SERAPHS. Celestial charges in armory denote dignity, glory, and honour. Guillim considers such charges should be borne by an ambassador, or by one who has been the bearer of joyful intelligence, and especially by one who has first planted religion in any country.

The CHERUB is represented as a human or angel's head, supported by a pair of wings, but the seraph possesses three pairs, the pair above the head and the pair beneath being crossed "in saltire," and there is one wing at each side of the head. Guillim adds, "Cherubims are above ordinary angels." Sir Thomas Chaloner *temp.* Charles I., bore on a black shield a chevron between three cherubims all of gold. This clearly indicates one who has performed high service for "the Church," not necessarily any established church, but probably for the "living Church" or the flock, which alone is to be valued.

> "O may I join the choir invisible
> Of those immortal dead who live again."
> —"GEORGE ELIOT."

ESTOILLES, or stars with six wavy points.
Guillim terms these the emblems of
God's goodness, or otherwise of
some eminence in the first bearer
above the ruder sort of men. The
Ingleby family bore on a black shield
an estoille of silver.

Estoille, or star of
six points.

The MULLET is a star of five points, and Guillim
holds that this is a falling or fallen star, not supposed
to be fallen from its high estate, but
to denote some Divine quality bestowed from above, whereby men
shine in virtue, learning, and works
of piety like bright stars on the
earth. If this figure is found pierced
with a round hole in the centre, it is no longer a

Three mullets, with
a fess humée.

Mullet, but a *Spur*. Of this rule there can be little
question, as I find that the ancient family of Spurre,
of Cornwall, bore a " Mullet pierced," as an evident
allusion to their name. A gold spur becomes the
dignity of knighthood, and a silver spur for that of
an esquire. (Guillim.) There was an ancient English
order entitled " Esquires of the Silver Spur," which
has been slightly revived in the present reign, and
such a creation affords a ready means of constituting
one as a legal esquire should he hold no office to
which such a title is affixed by usage.

The SUN. Guillim says this is the emblem of Glory and Splendour, and is the fountain of life.

The sun "in splendour."

Sloane Evans gives the meaning of this bearing to be "absolute authority." One ray of the sun signifies "By the light of Heaven." (See the arms of Aldam, Lesone, and De Fontibus, pages 150, 151 ; also remarks on De la Hays' arms, page 20.) Tertullian states that the Roman kings had their crowns constructed with points in the shape of the sun's beams, because they were themselves like suns and flaming lights ; for the whole world was led by their example.

The MOON was dedicated to the chaste Diana, and symbolised Serene power over mundane actions. The moon was said to bear that sovereignty by night which the sun bore by day.

"The dews of summer night did fall,
The moon, sweet *regent* of the sky,
Silvered the walls of Cumnor Hall
And many an oak that grew thereby."
—SCOTT'S *Kenilworth*.

The CRESCENT or increscent moon was said to signify one who has been "enlightened and honoured by the gracious aspect of his sovereign." It is also borne as the symbol of a "Hope of Greater Glory." In ancient days both the sun and moon were the objects of an adoration, of which some traces are still observable in various rites and customs through-out the world. Mr. Andrew Lang states that Diane de Poitiers bore as devices, crescents and bows and arrows, in allusion to her namesake Diana the huntress and goddess.

Crescent.

A Crescent and Mullet star of gold, on a green shield, form the ensign of the Turkish Empire, and as such was borne by the Saracens. The Minshuls of Cheshire, whose representative, Sir Michael de Minshul, was at the last Crusade in A.D. 1280, bore in their arms, especially conferred on Sir Michael, a crescent and star. The Hootons of Cheshire, who intermarried with the Minshuls, bore three stars or Mullets on a bend. British heraldry offers very numerous examples of the bearing of Crescents and Mullets, many of which bearings were undoubtedly derived from the Crusades. The Crescent and star are shown by D'Alviella to have been used together as symbols in Asia Minor and Egypt very many centuries before the Turkish conquests.

FIRE. The worship of fire was anciently con-nected with the universal worship of the sun. Guillim states that its bearing signifies Zeal. It would be difficult to find a more fitting symbol. One may be " consumed with zeal," as by fire !

LIGHTNING. This is said by Chassaneus to have been adopted as a device by Tomyris, Queen of Scythia. Guillim states that it signifies in armory the effecting of some weighty business with great celerity and force. The Roman Eagles were represented grasping in their claws a forked ray of lightning. D'Alviella shows that this is an extremely ancient symbol.

ROCKS signify, says Guillim, Safety, Refuge, and Protection.

The PORTCULLIS is considered in heraldry to signify an effectual protection in emergency, as it was used to guard the entrance to a fortress, and could be suddenly lowered against a surprise attack of the enemy, when there was no time for drawing up the drawbridge, or for closing and barricading the heavy doors. It was one of the badges of King Henry the Seventh, and is now borne on the arms of Westminster, and also by some private families. Henry derived this badge from the family of Beaufort, from which he was a descendant.

> " Up drawbridge, grooms. What, warder, ho !
> Let the portcullis fall !"

HUNTING HORN. This may have been adopted as a memento of the chase, and might signify one who is fond of high pursuits, as the chase was anciently reckoned, next to war, to be the most noble employment. The families of Forster and Forester, besides many others, bear hunting horns. It would be in keeping with the ancient symbolic spirit to suppose that this bearing means " Follow me, the hunt has begun !"

Hunting horn.

TRUMPET. Guillim says, "The sound of the trumpet is as the loud, far-reaching voice of the general, and encourages to the fight ; this therefore, with the *Drum* and *Fife*, which serve for the direction and encouragement of armies in the field, are emblems well becoming one who has bravely followed their sound in war. The symbolism therefore is a summons to be "ready for the fray." The ancient family of Trumpington bore two war-trumpets.

CANNON, MORTARS, CANNON BALLS, and GRENADES are well bestowed on those who have dared their terrors in sieges and battles. Sloane Evans states that the founder of one of the Welsh families, owning the name of Thomas, distinguished himself for his valour and skill, as First Master of Artillery, in the French wars under Edward III., and in consequence had awarded to him for arms a red shield bearing six cannon balls coloured gold. It is curious that these cannon balls should be coloured gold instead of black, which is the heraldic pellet or cannon ball.

The SWORD, Guillim remarks, is a weapon fitted for execution and justice, and he holds that it is the true emblem of military honour, and should incite the bearer to a just and generous pursuit of honour and virtue in warlike deeds. When borne with a cross in the same field it would signify the defence of the Christian faith. Elsewhere he refers to the Sword as signifying Government and Justice. The Cross of St. Paul consists of a cross-hilted sword, and it may be this that is intended in the arms of London, which latter consist of a white or silver shield bearing the red Cross of St. George of England, and in the dexter chief is a sword, which probably represents the Cross of the Patron Saint of London. These arms are of great antiquity, and under this supposition would form another instance of armorial symbolism at the earliest period. In Mr. Hewitt's "Ancient Armour" (London, 1860), reference is made to the London banner of the thirteenth century, which bore on it a sword as the emblem of St. Paul.

ARROWS and ARROW-HEADS. In the Scriptures arrows are sometimes referred to as emblems of affliction. Guillim affirms that the bearing of

arrow-heads is both ancient and honourable; of
Arrows, he says these are of the number of
weapons "destined to avengement," but he afterwards remarks that "*Bows* and *arrows* may signify
a man resolved to abide the uttermost hazard of
battle, who to that end has furnished himself to the
full." These may be taken to symbolise either
"Martial readiness," or, if with a cross, affliction.
In English arms the arrow points are usually shown
pointing downwards, but in France they reverse
this practice.

SPEAR or LANCE. The Romans regarding the
use of this weapon as exhibiting the perfection of
martial affairs, bestowed it only upon the valiant
and well-deserving soldier. It is the emblem of
knightly service, and would signify devotion to
honour. Spears are sometimes borne in allusion to
the crucifixion, together with other similar emblems.

SPEAR-HEADS or PHEONS. Guillim says of these
bearings, "Being apt and ready to pierce, according to some authors, they betoken a dexterity and
nimbleness of wit to penetrate and understand
matters of highest consequence." It would be
more in keeping with the meaning of all the other
similar charges, to ascribe the symbolism of these
to be "readiness for military service." Sir Philip
Sidney's paternal arms consisted of, on a gold

shield, one blue pheon, the point downwards.   The
Broad Arrow is derived from this emblem, although
Hargrave Jennings traces both to a very much
earlier symbol.

The SHIELD.   This, says Guillim, is the defence
and safeguard of soldiers in war, and serves to
honour them by depicting their armorial bearings
in time of peace.   It signifies "a Defender" when
borne of one plain colour in a coat of arms as a
special bearing or charge.   The shield is often
referred to in the Scriptures.

SADDLES and also STIRRUPS and SPURS would,
according to Guillim, signify preparedness for
active service.   The spur was also an emblem to
"press onward."

HORSE SHOE.   The well-known emblem of good
luck.   One of these was anciently considered to be
a sure safeguard against malign influences, and in
the rural parts of England, especially in Devon and
Cornwall, horse shoes may still be seen hung over
the doors of cottages and stables as safeguards
against evil spirits.   It has also been used as a
feudal tribute.

TRUNK OF A TREE.   This was anciently an object
of veneration.   D'Alviella states that among the
Hessians of the eighth century it was the *Simulacrum*
of the god Thor.

FUSIL. This is shaped very much like the lozenge, but is narrower and slightly longer. It has been stated to denote travel and labour. See also the Fusil of Yarn, page 116.

Three fusils gules conjoined in fess, on a shield argent.

MASCLE. This is of the shape of a lozenge, but "*Voided*," *i.e.* hollowed out in the centre, leaving only the rim of the figure. Guillim remarks, "This is the mesh of a net, which in Holy Writ is the hieroglyphic for persuasion, whereby men are induced to virtue and verity, and so may seem after some sort to be caught." Sir John Ferne says, they may signify, "*when borne in a red shield*, the bearer to have been most prudent and politic in the stratagems of war, for that colour is dedicated to Mars." "Therefore,"

A mascle argent, on a field sable.

adds Guillim, "the bearing of mascles is of greater honour than many other charges are, that in vulgar estimation are more accounted of." See further remarks on Frets, page 117.

SHACKLEBOLT (or *Fetterlock*). Guillim says, this, being one of the emblems of victory, is an honourable bearing in armory, and may well be borne by one who in the wars has taken his enemy prisoner, or for one who by his prowess can fetch off with

H

strength, or by his charity redeem, any of his fellow-soldiers in captivity. It is gene-rally used in armory with the latter signification. Sir Walter Scott represents Richard I. bearing the Shacklebolt as his device, when proceeding to the release of Ivanhoe. Nuthall, of Chester, bore

Fetterlock or shackle-bolt.

on a silver shield a shacklebolt coloured black. Anderton bore on a black shield two single shacklebolts and one double one, all of silver.

WATER BOUGETS are said to have been con-ferred on those who had brought water to an army or to a besieged place. They represent the ancient manner of carrying water in skins. Mr. Planché proves this

Water bougets.

conclusively.

CATHARINE WHEEL. This was said to have been used in the martyrdom of St. Catharine, and therefore it is the emblem of one who is pre-pared to undergo great trials for the Christian faith. It is rarely to be met with in armory.

ESCARBUNCLE. This is the symbol of supremacy, and is of great antiquity. It is generally accepted, says Sloane Evans, as representing a brilliant gem, the rays being shaped like sceptres. Some heralds have held that it is the large gemmed buckle of a belt used in war. This was the bearing of the kingdom of Navarre. It has been pointed out by Mr. Planché and various other authorities that the arms of Navarre probably represent a cross and a network of chains. The evidence as to this is certainly strong, but Planché gives an ancient drawing of the very early crest of John Plantagenet, Earl of Warren, which shows an unimpeachable escarbuncle standing out clearly above the helmet.

BUCKLES, in armory are considered ancient and honourable bearings, and signify victorious fidelity in authority. They are of various shapes, such as round, square, oval, and lozenge-shaped. They are borne by the ancient family of Hepburn, with the motto " Keep tryst."

MAUNCH or SLEEVE. This is a lady's sleeve of a very ancient pattern, and evidently became used in heraldry from the custom of the knights who attended tournaments wearing their ladies' sleeves as *gages d'amour* in the lists. It is a very ancient bearing in the De Mohun, De Mauley, and Hastings families. No particular meaning has been ascribed to it as a bearing, but we may feel sure that each knight that adopted it said, " For my lady's sake." This and many other tournament devices have been introduced into armory direct from the tourney lists, and probably because of their having been borne triumphantly in great tournaments.

The CLARION or REST.   The very nature of this bearing has been hotly disputed, and, to use an expression of Mr. Planché's, "has been the cause of much inkshed."   I think, however, that Planché has fully established the fact that this represents the ancient clarion, and that it was neither the rest for a lance, nor an organ "Sufflue."   If it be accepted as a clarion, it would have the same signification as the trumpet, before referred to.

BEACONS or CRESSETS.   Formerly each county possessed one or more beacons, in order to arouse all the country in the event of an invasion.   They signify one who is watchful for the commonwealth, or who gave the signal in time of danger.

CHAINS, when borne alone, or upon animals, represent a reward for acceptable and weighty service.   They are often conjoined with crowns and collars, and would mean that the bearer of such symbols had placed a chain of obligation on those whom he had bravely served.   For the same reason chains and collars are marks of honour in the orders of knighthood, as well as for sheriffs and mayors.

FUSIL OF YARN.   This is of a different form to the Fusil before referred to.   It is a hank of yarn with the spindle within, and is borne by the Trefusis—Lord Clinton's—family, evidently as an allusive bearing. It is of great antiquity. Morgan states that "Negotiation" is the meaning that has been assigned to this figure.

COVERED CUP. This charge is borne by the Butler family, in evident allusion to their family name, which latter again alludes to the office of king's butler, which is said to have been originally held by the head of this family. Other *Covered and open Cups* are sometimes representative of the Chalice used in the Communion or "the Mass," just as the Torteaux or red roundels borne by the Courtenays represent the Eucharistic "Manchet-cake" or wafer used in the Roman Catholic Church, and which alone, without the Chalice, is presented to the laity. Nisbet gives the arms of Lawrie of Maxwelltown, an open cup or goblet—evidently a chalice—out of which arises a chaplet between two laurel branches. The latter are evidently symbolical as well as allusive to the name. The branches of laurel point to a joyful triumph when coupled with the chaplet or crown of flowers, or this bearing may mean a cup overflowing with gladness.

The FRET has been termed "the heraldic true lover's knot." It consists of a mascle, behind or through which, two lines stand interlaced in the form of a saltire. This is really a bearing of nearly the same form as when a shield is borne "fretty," which latter is a lattice-work arrangement of interlaced pieces. A fretty shield consists

A fretty shield.

throughout of a series of apparent mascles, or meshes of a net, and Planché inclines to the belief that a net is intended by this armorial figure. Guillim's ruling as to the meaning of the net would still apply here, and, like the mascles, the fret or fretted shield would signify "Persuasion." When taken with the symbolism of the colours, such bearings are full of interest and dignity. We find in Froissart that the fret was so much valued, that in Edward III.'s French war, Lord Audeley conferred on his four chief followers his golden fret, to be borne within their arms, on a red ground, in memory of their great assistance to him in that war. Lord Audeley's own arms consisted of a red shield bearing a gold fret.

DIAPER. This is a fanciful tracery of lines on the shield, which was formerly used when representing arms on stained glass. These lines are formed of circles, squares, &c., within which were small flowers, stars, and other minute objects.

This tracery has caused some confusion to the decipherers of ancient bearings. The custom is again being revived in some modern heraldic paintings and book-plates. Great care should be used wherever diapering is employed, that there should be nothing suggestive of an heraldic charge in the design or execution of such lines. The word diaper comes from the word D'Ypres, where figured damask used to be made. Damask is derived from Damascus, whence the fabric was first obtained.

GAMMADION or *fylfot*. Planché cannot account for the origin of this figure, but said it is found introduced into heraldry at a very early period. D'Alviella, however, shows clearly that it is one of the earliest symbols of the world—as old as the Egyptian "flying disc"—and that it has travelled around the whole earth among all races, and from the very dawn of civilisation. It was, he says, the emblem of felicity. This zigzag decoration was constantly used by the Greeks in their costumes, architectural decorations, and pottery. It was used by the Chinese, Japanese, Thibetans, Hindoos, Celts, Franks, Saxons, Fins, and Romans, and by the Yucatans of North America, as well as by the Hittites, but curiously enough it is not met with either in Egypt, Assyria, or Chaldæa. Mr. Andrew

Lang asks, "Was it brought in a migration of which there is no evidence, or was it separately evolved?"

GUTTÉS or *drops*. These represent according to their colours various liquids, which are termed and signify as follows :—

Yellow	.	.	Gutté d'or	.	.	Drops of gold.
Blue	.	.	Gutté de larmes	.	Drops of tears.	
Green	.	.	Gutté d'olive	.	Drops of oil.	
White	.	.	Gutté d'eau	.	.	Drops of water.
Black	.	.	Gutté de poix	.	Drops of pitch.	
Red	.	.	Gutté de sang	.	Drops of blood.	

These guttés are sometimes used for the purpose of differencing" or "gerattyng," to which subject generally I have devoted some special remarks. I have found guttés borne in the following arms : Guillim exhibits the coat of Lemming, which consists of a silver shield sprinkled with drops of blood. This is evidently a symbolical bearing, referring to some sanguinary conflict in which its first bearer was engaged. The arms of Dannet were, a black shield, on which are drops of water. The arms of Roydenhall were, on a silver shield a red chief nebulée—that is, like a cloud—and the shield itself is sprinkled with drops of pitch. As we know that boiling pitch was often poured down upon the assailants of castles, I consider that this symbolism refers to its first bearer having performed a daring assault under a cloud of such drops rained down upon him. That the colour of this shield is white, and therefore shows one who delights in peace and sincerity, is no detraction to the martial endurance of its bearer. Such contrasts often occur in life as well as in armory. Another coat given by Guillim is that of Milketfield, which consists of a silver shield bearing a black engrailed cross, upon which are drops of gold. This shield being of silver, signifies Peace and Innocency, the black cross being *engrailed* signifies a constant faith while on *earth*, and the drops of gold might show spiritual riches derived from above. The meanings attached to these symbols by the ancient heralds would authorise such a translation of the above coats of arms. The following further examples are mentioned by Guillim and Papworth : Gold Guttés are borne by Lesington, Harbottle, and Crosbie ; gold with green guttés, by Grindoure ; white, by Cockshutt, and Boys ; red, by Thorndike ; black, by Gresque, of Lincoln. Fitz of Fitzford, Devon, bore on a silver shield a red cross, the shield semée or strewn with drops of blood. This extremely ancient shield is very symbolical of one who, possessing a peaceful disposition, had shed his blood for the Cross. St. Maur bore a shield of silver strewn with drops of tears and a black chevron "*Voided.*" I think this chevron, having been represented as voided or open, shows some great work unaccomplished, and that the bearer deplored his unavailing efforts. Mr. Lower mentions that the Duke of Anjou, when king of Sicily, is said to have originated the bearing of drops of tears. He appeared at a tournament after the loss of his kingdom bearing a black shield, on which were depicted drops to represent tears, thus indicating his grief and his loss. This, however, was merely his tournament device, and not his permanent armorial bearing. Mr. Andrew Lang states that Henry III. of France decorated his sumptuously bound volumes with emblems of the Passion, and with tears.

ROUNDLES. The old heralds have attached various names and significations to these round figures. When of gold they were called Bezants, and represented ancient Byzantine coins. This bearing has been said to denote "one who had been found worthy of trust and treasure." The white roundle is called a *Plate*, and denoted "generosity." The green was called a *Pomme*, and had the same signification as the apple; when purple it was called a *Golpe*, and "denoted a wound"; when blue it was "a *Hurt* or wortleberry"; when black it was "a *Pellet, Ogress*, or *Gunstone*," and represented a cannon ball ; when red it was called *Torteau*, and signified the communion wafer or " Manchet-cake " ; when Tawney it was called an *Orange*, and *signified a tennis-ball.* Such are the terms generally applied by our ancient heralds, who in this respect are often in agreement. It is needless for us to find fault with the quaint names of many of these figures, although we cannot help being amused by their simplicity. If heraldry had been constructed in our own day, I have no doubt that its terms and figures would all have been perfectly devised in the manner of an exact science, without any doubtful or confusing marks, or amusing freaks of terminology.

The FOUNTAIN. Before leaving the subject of roundles, I should refer to this figure, which is also considered to be one of the roundles. It is represented crossed with wavy bars of blue and white in order to represent water. It signifies a fountain or spring, and with this intent is borne in the ancient arms of Stourbridge, in reference to the sources of the river Stour. It is also to be found in the arms of a family named Welles.

The WHIRLPOOL is a circular voluted figure occupying the whole of the shield. This was borne by the ancient family of Gorges, of Devon.

The WHEEL is the emblem of Fortune. The *winged wheel* was anciently used as a symbol of motion among the Greeks. (D'Alviella's " Migration of Symbols.")

The CORNUCOPIA or Horn of Plenty is the ancient symbol of the bounty of Nature's gifts, and would possess the same signification in heraldry. It has been used in England as a crest, and is borne in the arms of Peru.

CHAPLETS and WREATHS. These have been worn of various kinds from the earliest times. A wreath of wild olives was the reward of the Olympic games, of laurel leaves in the Pythian, of parsley in the Nemean, and of pine-twigs in the Isthmic games. The Romans gave a wreath of grass to in-

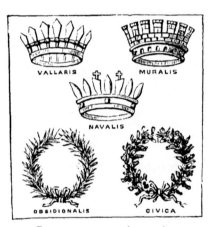

Roman crowns and wreaths.

dividual soldiers who had performed a deed of special valour in the field. This was supposed to be made of grass plucked from the field of battle. Goodall, of Suffolk, bore a "chaplet Graminy" of green on a white Canton, in the arms granted to him in 1612. This was evidently a grant for special service in the field.

The TRIUMPHAL WREATH was composed of laurel leaves accompanied with berries. The laurel was consecrated by the Romans to Apollo. A laurel wreath was worn in token of victory by the Roman emperors during their magnificent triumphal entries into Rome. (Guillim.)

LAUREL LEAVES. Guillim says that these leaves were considered in ancient times as remedies against poison, and were used as tokens of peace and quietness. Two green laurel branches are borne by Swanson, and doubtless were adopted in memory of some great triumph. Two branches of laurel crossed in saltire, between four pheons, are borne in the arms of Byam, of Somersetshire. Here we find the emblems of triumph and war are borne together. Laurel branches were held in honour in the temples of ancient Greece.

The CIVIC WREATH was of oak leaves and acorns, tied together with a ribbon. It was given to him who saved a brother citizen's life, but in modern times it has been ascribed emblematically to one who has shown the larger civic virtue of patriotism in defence of his native land or of its possessions beyond the sea. It might, in the future, well be awarded to any one who shall in any way uphold, or help to unite, the great confederated empire of Britain.

The FLORAL CHAPLET is generally shown with

green leaves, and with four roses at equal distances from each other. It is the crown of joy, and award of admiration.

> "This glory garland round my soul."
> —ROBERT BROWNING.

GARLANDS of FLOWERS were worn at weddings, festivals, and feasts in that springtime of the world, the ancient Classic times. The wreath was often worn around the neck, in order that the scent of the flowers might be fully enjoyed.

In a grant of arms to Trout, of Devon, in 1588, the Armada year, is a lion rampant, holding in his dexter paw a green chaplet. This evidently refers to some daring deed by which victory was attained. In the ancient arms of a family named Conqueror, is a laurel wreath between three pheons. Here we have the emblem of the victor, doubtless referring also to the name, together with the symbols of warfare. The arms of Faulder show three green chaplets, which are entwined with red roses. I have no doubt that the original bearer performed some splendid services, possibly in behalf of the house of Lancaster, or of some other Royal house. Ralph, Lord of Gormethorpe in A.D. 1301, bore Barry of eight pieces, silver and blue, and three chaplets of red roses. He was son and heir of William Fitz Ralph, by Joan de Greystocke. He afterwards took the latter name. These chaplets and bars were borne by his ancestors the Fitz Ralphs, and by his descendants the Greystockes. As these chaplets were borne *before* the Wars of the Roses, I assume that possibly they may have been assumed in reference to some tournament victory. Nisbet quotes an ancient Latin writer, who says that all flowers are the symbols of hope, but they are oftener used as emblems of joy. The College of Arms records the grant in 1767 to Sutton, of Westminster, of the following coat: On a silver shield a wreath of oak acorned "proper," *i.e.* in natural colours, and on a blue chief a twisted serpent of gold and a white dove, each looking towards the other. Was Coventry Patmore thinking of this device when he wrote the following verse in "The Angel in the House"?

> "Love, kissed by wisdom, wakes twice love,
> And wisdom is, though loving, wise.
> Let Dove and Snake, and Snake and Dove,
> This wisdom's be, that love's device."

OAK TREE, ACORNS, and OAK LEAVES. The Oak holds the first place amongst trees, and is said to signify Antiquity and Strength. Wreaths of oak leaves were consecrated to Jupiter, and the tree itself was held sacred by the Greeks. A great deal might be written about the sacred trees of antiquity, including the "Tree of Life" and the "Tree of Knowledge." Certain trees have been held in high veneration from the earliest time, both in Europe and Asia. The ash was particularly venerated by the Saxons.

The ancient family of Trelawney of Trelawne, Cornwall, bear three oak leaves. The family of Bray, of Cornwall, bear three oak trees, on which are golden acorns. Viscount Lismore bears in his arms a mountain, on the left side of which is a hurst or grove of oak trees, from which a wolf is issuing. Some ancient family tradition is evidently here referred to. Bishop Majendie, of Chester, bore a green mount, on which was a tree between a serpent erect on the dexter side, and a dove on the sinister. This reminds one of the coat of Sutton, to which I have just referred, and possibly it was this coat which suggested Patmore's lines. The scriptural allusion to the wisdom of the serpent and innocence of the dove may have been intended in both this and Sutton's arms. The family of Montefiore bear a *Cedar tree* between two mounts of flowers. The mounts of flowers evidently refer to the name. This coat is a modern grant. The cedar tree would appear to point to the ancient Judæan origin of this celebrated family. The cedars of Lebanon are scripturally referred to as being emblems of stately beauty, and they were carved as symbols within the Temple of Solomon.

OLIVE BRANCH or LEAVES are the emblems of Peace and Concord. The Dove brought back an olive branch to Noah. The family of Vanhatton, of London,—descended from Holland,—bear two olive branches in their arms.

The PALM is the emblem of Victory, Justice, and Royal honour. All the victorious princes in olden time when returning in triumph from mighty enterprises bore palm branches. David wrote, "The righteous shall flourish as the palm-tree." In armory the palm branch is often used as the symbol of a victor. Two green palm branches are borne in the arms of Stanger. Farnwell, of Gloucester, bears a lion seated, holding in both paws a palm branch. Montgomery, of Broom-lands, related to the family of the Earl of Eglinton, bore on a blue shield a branch of palm between three fleur-de-lis, all of gold. The palm branch differs this coat from the Earl of Eglinton's, which latter is exactly the same as the arms of the Bourbons. Nearly sixty years ago the Earl of Eglinton held at Eglinton Castle the last tournament that Britain can expect to behold. It was a very remarkable assembly.

I

The CYPRESS, PINE, and YEW are held to be emblematical of Death, but D'Alviella states that among the Egyptians these evergreen trees symbolised Hope in an eternal life beyond the tomb.

Fir twigs were consecrated by the Romans to the Fauns and Silvans. The Scotch family of Walkinshaw bore, on a mount a grove of firs. Three pine-trees were borne by the families of Kempthorne and Lee, of Cornwall. Three Cypress sprigs were borne by the name of Birkin.

The PINE CONE is stated by Count D'Alviella to have been an emblem of "Life," amongst the ancient Semitic races, the same as was the Crux Ansata or key-cross among the Egyptians.

ACACIA branches or leaves signify Eternal and affectionate remembrance.

WOODBINE LEAVES are, says Guillim, the type of love, which injures nothing it clings to.

IVY LEAVES. Morgan gives their definition to be "Strong and lasting friendship — *Neque mors separabit.*" The Ivy and Vine were by the Romans consecrated to Bacchus, the Myrtle to Venus, the Poplar to Hercules, Wheat-ears to Ceres, and Reeds to the river gods. Papworth gives an instance of the bearing of three tufts of reeds by the family of Sykes, while he states that Tilsey, of Yorkshire, bore tufts of grass, and Mallerby, of Devon, a bunch of nettles. The latter bearing was evidently allusive to the name of the bearer.

BAY LEAVES. It is generally understood that the wreath of bay was that which was anciently conferred on the poet, and it is also applicable to other distinguished·writers, but Mr. Grant Allen considers that the bay was in ancient times the victor's laurel. Modern usage has established the distinction here stated. The Chane family bore three branches of bay, and Foulis, of Edinburgh, bore a holly branch between three bay leaves. (Papworth.)

HOLLY. This evergreen was used to adorn temples and sacred places, and its name is derived from the word holy. Morgan says, these leaves are emblems of truth. The family of Irvine bears three holly branches, and another branch of this family bears three bundles of holly. I have just referred to the holly branch borne by Foulis.

The BROOM plant or PLANTA GENISTA is the emblem of humility, and was the badge of the Plantagenet family, who probably derived their surname from their badge, as was the case of many others who had adopted striking cognisances, before the surname had become settled as an affix to the Christian name. Papworth gives a very singular coat, borne by the name of Brander,

which shows on a chief a *burning bush* on the
top of a mountain, and between two white roses.
There are also three lions borne below in the
shield. It would be interesting to discover what
incident in the first bearer's life, originated this
singular device. Papworth states that Dr. Lopus,
physician to Queen Elizabeth, bore in 1591 a
Pomegranate tree with golden fruit.

The POMEGRANATE fruit is, according to D'Alviella,
the symbol of fertility and abundance. It is borne
in the arms of Granada, and was used as a badge
by Katharine of Aragon. Henry VIII. bore this
badge "impaled" or divided with his own badge
of a rose, at various tournaments.

APPLES, PEARS, and OTHER FRUIT, Morgan says,
signify Liberality, Felicity, and Peace.

The WHEAT GARB or SHEAF, says Guillim,
signifies "Plenty," and "that the first bearer did
deserve well for his hospitality." It is, however,
held by other writers to mean that the "Harvest
of one's hopes" had been secured, and I hold that
this, the higher symbolism, should, by Guillim's own
ruling, be accepted here.

WHEAT-EARS, in the Scriptures, are referred to
as emblems of the faithful, and were probably so
intended when first borne in arms.

The RED ROSE, according to the old poets,

signified and expressed " Beauty and grace," and is reckoned the first amongst flowers. The old name of Rosamund signifies " Rose of the world." As before stated, all flowers are held to be typical of Hope, and also of Joy.

The WHITE ROSE was the type of Love and Faith.

There can be no doubt that the frequent use of roses in English armory is greatly due to the adoption of the badges of the red and white rose in the Wars of the Roses, but a yellow or golden rose is found in the arms of Cossington, and also in Umfraville's. A lion bearing a green rose is borne by Trant, of Devon. A red rose is borne by Beverley, while another branch of the Beverleys bear a " counterchanged coat," which gives the rose half red and half white. This would have been a safe bearing during the " Wars of the Roses" ! A rose and thistle conjoined are borne by Ashton, and also by Bispham. A thistle is borne by Leslie, Earl of Melville, and one crowned with an imperial crown, is borne by the name of Leven. A single rose is the mark of Cadency for the seventh son, but it is then represented as a small figure. Count D'Alviella states that the Rosette was a solar symbol among the most ancient races. The red rose was borne above the white by Henry VII. after his marriage with the "White Rose of York."

The LILY is the emblem of Purity, or "whiteness of soul," and by the Roman Catholic Church was ascribed to be the special emblem of the Virgin Mary. Ferdinand, king of Spain, instituted a special order under the name of the Lily. It is borne in arms under various colours. Some

writers have derived the armorial lily from the Egyptian lotus, but the fleur-de-lis is undoubtedly a golden lily. It is borne in the French arms on a blue shield,—blue being the colour ascribed to the Virgin,—so that the "Most Catholic country,"— one of whose kings was canonised as St. Louis,—bore a thoroughly emblematical armorial ensign.

Ancient arms of France, a shield strewn with lilies; the number of the latter was afterwards reduced to three.

Three lilies with stalks slipped, *proper*—that is, of natural colours—were borne by the name of Beauty. On a red shield, three pots of lilies, all coloured white, were borne by the name of Wain, of Scotland. Many similar bearings of the garden lily are to be found, besides the innumerable bearings of the heraldic lily or fleur-de-lis. A large number of the latter bearings exist in English armory, having direct reference to the early French wars, in which their original assumers had been engaged.

The TREFOIL, or three-leaved grass, is frequently used in heraldry. This is the *Shamrock*, and Guillim says it signifies Perpetuity, or that the just man shall never wither. It is the floral device of Ireland.

QUATREFOIL. This, says Nichols, signifies the Primrose, which of all other flowers brings good tidings of spring, and signifies good luck to the finder. Primroses are borne by the Earl of Rosebery, in allusion to the family patronymic, unless the surname of Primrose first arose on account of the armorial bearings of the family, which is a very ancient one.

CINQUEFOILS. Like all other flowers these signify Hope and Joy. Cinquefoils were held by the ancient heralds to represent the following flowers, according to the colours in which they happened to be borne: The yellow cinquefoil was the Primrose; the white represented the Jessamine; the red was the Rose; the blue was the Periwinkle; the black, the "Dawle"; the green, the five-leaved grass; the purple, the Buglass, the Tawney, the Stock Gilly-flower—"July-flower"; and the Sanguine, the Poppy. A *Six-foil* is borne in the arms of D'Arcy. The Huitfoil is the mark of Cadency for the ninth son. The French heralds simply named the colour of each cinquefoil without ascribing it to be any particular flower, and this course is followed by all other modern heralds.

MARIGOLD or "Golden Mary." This flower, Morgan states, was the emblem of Devotion and Piety. I do not know of any instance of its being borne in heraldry.

PINKS and CARNATIONS are often borne in arms, and signify Admiration. I think that most of the floral heraldic bearings were first adopted as tournament devices, and afterwards continued as armorial emblems. The following instances may be noted of various floral arms, and a very large number more could easily be recorded in British and foreign heraldic collections : A Sunflower was borne by Count Florio of Spain, granted in 1614, two purple Columbines by Bessell; three green Columbines by Cadman; two Gilly-flowers by Wade, of York, and three by Wade, of Warwickshire; three red Carnations, with green stalks and leaves, by Noyce; two Pinks by another branch of the Wade family; three red Daisies—*i.e.* Day's eyes—by Deisie, of Scotland; three Narcissuses by the Earl of Cavan; three Poppy heads on their stalks, all of gold, by Boller; and the before-mentioned Primroses by the Earl of Rosebery's family. Daisies, and especially the garden varieties, are often used as devices for the name of Margaret or Marguerite. Mr. Andrew Lang mentions that Queen Marguerite de Valois placed daisies on her book-covers. Margaret, Countess of Richmond, and mother of Henry VII., also adopted the same device.

A curious bearing is that of Alten, namely, on a white shield, a bend of red roses and red lozenges, alternately disposed. I think that Constancy to the Red-rose seems evidently to be alluded to in this shield, since the lozenge was the emblem of Constancy.

It is singular that no instance occurs of the bearing of the Pansy or the Violet in English armory. One would have thought that the " Pansy for thoughts," and "Violets dim, but sweeter than the lids of Juno's eyes, or Cytherea's breath," would have appealed as strongly as any other flowers, to the fervently poetic minds of the knights of the tourney, who seemed to have been so conscious that they were living in a romantic and poetic age. A work, which I have not had the pleasure of seeing, was published a good many years ago on the "Flowers in Heraldry." It has become exceedingly scarce. My examples are from " Burke's Armory" and " Papworth's Ordinary."

CROWNS, MITRES, EPISCOPAL HATS, &c.

I HAVE before stated that the meaning of the Crown, when borne within the shield of arms, is either Royal or Seigniorial authority, but there are a great variety of crowns and coronets to be found used as crests, or as emblems of dignity, beneath the crests, besides Episcopal Mitres and hats with tassels, borne by Cardinals, Archbishops, Bishops, and Abbots. The tasselled hats *do not all pertain to Cardinals*, unless they are of scarlet, as hats of other colours may belong to Roman Catholic Archbishops and Bishops who may choose to employ them in place of the Mitre. The rule is as follows : They are of red for Cardinals, of green for Archbishops, and black for Bishops, Abbés, and Prothonotaries. The number of the tassels has been varied from time to time.

When a crown or coronet is borne upon the shield as an heraldic charge, it is invariably so placed with a symbolic intent, which may either have reference to the acquisition or defence of some earthly crown, or to the hope of inheriting one in a brighter and happier world !

The CHAPEAU or Cap of Maintenance is some-times borne as a charge in the shield, but oftener underneath the crest. Every text-book on heraldry supplies the distinc-tions observed with regard to the bearing of variously designed

Chapeau.

helmets, together with their owners' crests, and also as to the rule respecting supporters. Every one is permitted to display a "*mantling*" with his arms if he chooses to do so. This mantling appears to represent the original *coat of arms*, as it now takes its colours from those of the shield, and, in some instances—where it is shown turned back at the sides—we find charges from the shield reproduced upon the mantling. The tabard of the heralds-at-arms continues to be *an actual coat of arms.*

The LAMBREQUIN was a kind of hood worn around the helmet, and this is represented flow-ing off from the helmet, and surmounted by the crest.

The HELMET itself, as a bearing within the shield, is held to denote Wisdom and surety in defence.

SUPPORTERS are of an infinite variety, and I may mention just a few of these.

HOPE. A female figure, richly attired, resting one hand upon an anchor.

TRUTH. A female figure in white, with head irradiated, on her breast a sun, and in her right hand a mirror.

FORTITUDE is clad in a corselet of scale-armour, on her head a plumed casque, her right hand bears a bunch of oak, and her left arm rests on a pillar.

JUSTICE holds in her right hand a naked sword erect, and in the left hand a pair of scales.

MERCY bears the sword in a reversed position.

PRUDENCE holds a javelin — or sometimes a mirror—entwined with a serpent.

LIBERALITY bears the Cornucopia.

FAME is represented blowing a trumpet.

That all these virtues are represented by *female* emblematical figures, bestows a richly deserved compliment on the fair sex.

Among other supporters are soldiers, savages, tritons, and numerous chimerical figures of gods and monstrous beasts, besides a whole menagerie of ordinary animals and birds. The original idea of a supporter appears to have been the representation of a figure *holding up* the shield of arms. In

Maspero's "Dawn of Civilisation" is an engraving of a singular device in stone, which was excavated in Nineveh, and which very closely resembles a complete coat of arms, with a crest and two supporters. This is doubtless an accidental resemblance.

Count D'Alviella in his "Migration of Symbols" remarks as follows: "Then chivalry placed its coats of arms between the two creatures facing one another—lions, leopards, unicorns, griffins, giants, &c. Charles Lenormant was not mistaken in saying, with respect to the affiliation of these types, 'When the use of armorial bearings began to develop in the West, Europe was deluged with manufactured articles of Asia, and the first lions drawn on escutcheons were certainly copied from Persian and Arabian tissues. These tissues themselves dated back from one imitation to another, to the models from which, perhaps over a thousand years before Christ, the author of the bas-reliefs of Mycenæ drew his inspiration.'"

BADGES or Cognisances. These bearings,—often confounded with family crests, — are heraldic figures adopted at various times or on special occasions, by royal personages or military commanders. The Roses of York and Lancaster, the Thistle of Scotland, and the Trefoil or Shamrock of Ireland, are among the best-known instances. A work by Mrs. Bury Pallisser, entitled " Historic Badges and War-cries," deals very fully with this subject, and in the work before cited by Mr. Planché,—the " Pursuivant of Arms,"—are some learned chapters on the subject, especially treating on the badges adopted from time to time by the English royal houses. The critical ability which this author has displayed in dealing with this subject, entitles him to the gratitude and admiration of all heraldic students.

CRESTS. I have only incidentally referred to this branch of heraldry. The crest was worn by the knight on his helmet, who often thus reproduced the chief charge in his coat or shield of arms. This process, however, was sometimes reversed in practice, as during the growth of heraldry the crest which had been borne on the helmet was sometimes also adopted as the sole armorial bearing. This was, however, very rarely practised, and heralds generally prefer the study of the shield of arms, and pay much less attention to crests, badges, and supporters.

The MURAL CROWN (page 124) was of gold, adorned with battlements, and was given by the Romans to him who first mounted the breach in the walls of a besieged town or fortress. It is also applicable to the defender of a fortress, or as a token of civic honour.

The NAVAL CROWN (page 124) was of gold, and ornamented with the prows and sterns of ancient galleys. This was usually awarded to the one who first boarded an enemy's ship. It is sometimes now awarded in the arms of distinguished naval commanders.

TORCH. An inverted torch borne on a tomb indicates the extinction of the family of the person commemorated. The ordinary bearing of a torch in arms is for a zealous man who has engaged in some signal service. Collins, of Devon, bears three torches, and Collens, apparently another branch of the same family, bore three firebrands.

> " I told her of the knight that wore
>   Upon his shield a burning brand ;
> And that for ten long years he woo'd
>   The lady of the land."
>   —S. T. COLERIDGE.

The SPHERE possesses a geographical or scientific reference. Archimedes is said to have directed that one should be engraved on his tomb.

FLINT STONES and STEEL. These ancient means for producing fire have been borne as denoting readiness for zealous service. John, Earl of Flanders used as a device a flint stone and steel.

His son Philip the Good founded the order of the Golden Fleece, the collar of which order bears flint stones and steels.

MEN and WOMEN are often borne in the shield of arms, as well as in the crest, or as supporters to the shield. The symbolisms of such bearings are decipherable in many ways, but some of these cannot now be even a matter for speculation. *Moors* or *Moors' heads,* as I mentioned before, are supposed generally to refer to conflicts with the Saracens. The crest of the Ellis family is a naked female, with her tresses dishevelled around her shoulders. The arms of Drummond, of Scotland, show on a gold shield three bars wavy of blue, over all a naked man swimming and holding a sword in his right hand, coloured in natural colours. Grimsditch, of Chester, bore, *temp.* Henry III., on a green shield a red griffin seizing a man in complete armour, who is lying on his back. Campidon bore on his shield the half-figure of a woman crowned with an antique crown, with her neck and shoulders bare. The origins of these strange arms are entirely unknown.

Wirgman, of London, bore on a blue shield a female figure representing Justice, habited in white, holding in her right hand a pair of scales, and in her left a sceptre, both of gold. In this instance a sceptre is borne instead of a sword. I consider that this bearing memorialises a signal act of justice performed by some queen in behalf of the first bearer of the arms.

A MOLE is borne by both the Twistletons and the Mitfords. A *Rat* occurs in the crest of the Dawsons. A *Seal* is borne by Fennor, of Sussex. A *Monkey* is borne as a crest, with two monkeys as supporters, by the Fitzgeralds. No symbolism has been attached to these bearings, and the reason for their adoption is unknown. Their first assumers may, however, have intended to express the meaning of the motto of the ancient Holt family, of Aston Hall, Birmingham, "Exaltavit humiles."

A LAMB'S FLEECE is appropriately borne by the Jason family.

The TENT or PAVILION was another of the emblems of readiness for martial employment. "To your tents, O Israel!" In the accompanying engraving the pavilion itself bears within it, the Tudor royal arms of England and France, borne quarterly.

The HOUR-GLASS is the emblem of the flight of time and of man's mortality. It is borne in several British coats of arms.

K

A Book, if open, signifies Manifestation, and if closed, Counsel.   (Morgan's "Sphere of Gentry.")

Insects.   The only symbolisms that have been attached to any one of these besides the Grass-hopper, Ant, and Bee, referred to previously, is to the *Butterfly*, the Greek emblem of Psyche, or the Soul.   This is occasionally borne in heraldry. The Ant is borne by Kendiffe, the Bee by Bolowre, and the Hornet by another branch of the latter family.   The Gadfly has been borne in armory, and also as a device by De Thou, according to Mr. Fletcher in his monograph on book bindings.

Pilgrims' Wallets and Palmers' Staves have been borne in reference to early pilgrimages to Jerusalem.   Nisbet gives the arms of Lamb of Duncam, as consisting of three pilgrims' staves.

Passion Nails are borne in token of poignant suffering undergone by the first bearer.   The family of Wishart bear three red passion nails. Three black passion nails piercing a red human heart were borne by the Logans, descended from Sir R. Logan, who accompanied Lord James Douglas to Jerusalem with the heart of King Robert Bruce.   The crowned heart of the Douglases, and the fetterlock and heart of Lockhart, are said to have been derived from the same devoted pil-grimage.

BELLS are occasionally borne in arms, and signify the supposed power of church bells to disperse evil spirits in the air, and as to their invocation of guardian saints and angels. A *Hawk's bells* would denote one who feared not to signalise his approach in either peace or war. Hewlett, in his "Armour of the Middle Ages," states that bells were sometimes worn on the horses used at tournaments.

KEYS are often borne as emblems of guardianship and dominion, chiefly in connection with the Roman Church, with special reference to St. Peter. The ancient arms of the See of Rome show the keys crossed, being then called the "keys of life and death," but the Crux Ansata of the ancient Egyptians also represented the "key of life." Rome borrowed much of its symbolism from the banks of the Nile.

MUSICAL PIPES and TABORS are emblems of festivity and rejoicing. One cannot help recalling here the annoyance caused to gentle Diana Vernon, by Frank Osbaldistone's reference to the pipes in her paternal arms as being, as he supposed, "penny whistles." (*Vide* "Rob Roy," chapter x.)

" Heard melodies are sweet, but those unheard
    Are sweeter ; therefore, ye soft pipes, play on ;
    Not to the sensual ear."
                                    —KEATS.

FLAGS and BANNERS borne on the shield, or
as crests, are usually adopted in reference to some
special action in which they have been captured,
or otherwise as a signal reward for gallant service.
They are also sometimes found borne with religious
emblems.   Papworth gives the coat of Garbett, A.D.
1486, a red shield bearing upon it a knight's banner
of white, flowing to the dexter side, and on which
is an Imperial Eagle.

MOTTOES.   Another interesting feature in connection with the study of heraldry occurs in the
great variety of mottoes which are to be found in
collections of arms or of heraldic book-plates.
These mottoes sometimes represent the ancient
war-cries of historic families, or they may point
to a sentiment of loyalty or of personal devotion,
to some aspiration for worldly advancement, or
speak of a hope extending beyond a transitory
life.   A number of these, too, are found to refer
either to the armorial symbols, or to the names
of their bearers.   In many modern book-plates,
a favourite verse from an admired poet, is often
added to various pictorial designs surrounding
the shield of arms.   It is not my duty to deal
with the above fascinating side of armorial devices.

EXAMPLES OF SYMBOLISMS OF COLOURS AND ARMORIAL BEARINGS

A FEW further examples of symbolic charges and colours may be here given, in illustration of the manner in which arms may be translated. A good number of very ancient coats of arms were borne composed simply of two colours divided by lines of various kinds. Such arms would be perfectly meaningless but for the symbolism of the colours themselves. The following are a few instances :—
The arms of Waldegrave, silver and red parted *per pale*. This shield means, readiness for the delights of peace or the martial acts of war. The Birminghams, created in A.D. 1316 Lords of Athenry, in Ireland, bore gold and red, parted per pale indented, that is, by an indented line in the form of a pale. The meaning here evidently is, that the bearer wished to typify a generous and elevated mind, which had borne the fiery ordeal of war.

The ancient family of Zusto, of Venice, bore gold and blue, parted *per fess*, that is, a line in the place of the fess. Here we have typified a

generous and elevated spirit combined with a loyal
disposition. Any religious emblem borne on a
blue shield, or blue portion of the shield, would
possess particular significance, azure being the
colour ascribed by the Roman Church to the
Virgin Mary. Guillim describes a coat parted *per
bend* green and gold. This simply means hope
and loyalty in love, combined with a generous
and elevated mind. The arms of Aston were,
black and silver parted *per chevron*. Here we have
Constancy, with Peace and Sincerity.

Another coat given by Guillim is gyronny of
six, blue and ermine. This white fur would be
reckoned to symbolise the same as the colour
white or silver, but the fur is an extra note of
dignity. The meaning of this coat is Loyalty, with
Peace and Sincerity, and the gyrons are said to
be typical of Unity.

Among other ancient bearings of symbolisms,
I may instance the following from my collection
of numbers of such instances :—

On a red shield, and in the "chief" or topmost
part, a silver cloud, from which the sun's "resplen-
dent rays" are issuing. Borne by Lesone, of North-
amptonshire. This is not a mere "canting coat,"
because the clouds and simply the sun's rays would
be unnecessary if the bearer wished only to repre-

sent a sun. The red shield points to military service, and the clouds to arduous difficulties overcome.

On a blue shield, from the right corner of which issues one golden ray of the sun, borne by the name of Alden. There can be no doubt that these bearers adopted the sun's rays as being highly symbolical. In the latter instance, Loyalty or Truth is expressed by the colour of the shield.

On a blue shield, on which are the sun and moon above seven stars, all of gold, borne by Johannes de Fontibus, sixth Bishop of Ely. This coat has evidently a scriptural symbolism.

A shield crossed by nebulée bars of black and gold, representing clouds, borne by Lord Montjoy and Earl of Devon, *temp*. Elizabeth. This coat represents clouds with a gold and not with a " silver lining," and doubtless refers to a glorious deliverance from poignant suffering or impending disaster.

On an ermine shield, a red rose; the arms of Beverley. Here we have an ermine " coat," dignified by the bearing of the " queen of the garden " as its sole emblem. The roses borne in the arms of Lord Abergavenny were placed there by his ancestor Richard Neville, Earl of Warwick, better known as the " King-maker."

On a silver shield, and upon a red chevron three white skulls, borne by the name of Bolter.

Here the shield gives " Peace," but the red chevron might refer to the performance of some considerable work with military fortitude, and in the face of death thrice dared.

On a red shield three Paschal lambs, each with staff, cross, and banner, all of silver; borne by the family of Rowe, of Devon, now represented by Mr. J. Brooking-Rowe, F.S.A. Here is indicated a warrior who, having engaged himself in the defence of the Church, bears one of its principal symbols, thrice repeated in memory of the Trinity.

On a silver shield, and upon a green bend, between six red crosslets fitchée, that is, sharpened at the lower end, three golden crosiers; borne by Wear, of Wear Gifford, Devon. Here the Peace symbolised by the shield, and Hope by the bend, is appropriately connected with the emblems of the "Good Shepherd" of the Church, and the crosses of Faith.

Sir Edward Maunsell bore on a silver shield a black tower with a golden ladder resting against it. Some might say that it was gold alone which had won this castle, but it is certain that the worthy knight would never have borne any such attributable device. I would suggest that it denoted that a golden service had been performed by the capture of a fortalice.

The student of armory will experience no difficulty

in finding an endless number of symbolical coats of arms, similar to those which I have just described.

The reader—if he or she shall have accompanied me thus far—will have surveyed a wide field of inquiry, in which the symbols, or imaged ideas, of many ages of mankind have been appealed to in connection with the bearing of armorial devices. My purpose in writing this treatise will have been achieved if I have succeeded in proving that in many a coat of arms, found either on a church window, carved stone, or book-plate, may perhaps lie hidden, in cryptic symbols, interesting reference to some action or aspiration of its first possessor, or of his feudal alliance with some historic chieftain, or again, perhaps marking his connection with a distant country, which had been the cradle of his ancient race. I have tried to maintain that the ancient bearing of armorial devices had generally a symbolical intent; and that many of such symbols had really been inherited by mediæval heraldry from that remote earlier age " when the world was young," at which time symbols were used, as Sir George Birdwood observes, to express " the unseen realities of human life."

A coat of arms showing the manner in which the arms of a man and his wife are borne impaled in one shield. In this case, both of the arms possessed borders around them, but these are cut off at the division line of " impalement."

CADENCY AND DIFFERENCING

BOTH of these subjects are classed by ancient writers under the latter name, and I now merely refer to this subject so far as appears to be necessary in considering the reasons assignable for the various bearings in a particular coat of arms. The late Mr. J. G. Nichols in his " Herald and Genealogist," in referring to this subject, says, " Differencing comprises the growth and ramifications of coat armour, and the whole system of its early development has been strangely lost sight of." I propose to make use of a few notes which I have taken of the remarks of several ancient and modern writers who have dealt with this question. In an able work by Francis Nichols, published early in the last century—and to which I have before made several references—the following interesting statements occur : " These Differences were invented with the intent that coat armour might descend to posterity with safety and free from strife, and with us in Britain there has been a *threefold difference* observed, which are those of chiefs of families,

consanguinity, and strangers. The Difference for
the chiefs are the Label or Border, the first being
sometimes charged and sometimes plain, the Border
either plain, charged, compound, quarterly, engrailed,
or indented ; *all of which are differences for eldest sons.*
The Differences for consanguinity are a Crescent for
the second son, a Mullet for the third, the Martlet or
footless swallow for the fourth, an Annulet for the
fifth, and a Fleur-de-lis for the sixth son, all of which
are called Differences of kinsmen, because they serve
to show those who are descended from one and the
same stock. Thirdly, the Differences of strangers
are, Barrulets, Bends, Chevrons, pales, and quarters."
To these may be added from Guillim, Orles, Cotises,
and Bendlets, besides a variety of charges, such
as Billets, Escallops, Goutés, Trefoils, Quatrefoils,
Cinquefoils, besides Crosslets and other small bearings. When these small objects were sprinkled over
the shield, it was called " gerattyng," according to
Dame Berners. Speaking of the varieties of Differences which have been used from time to time,
Guillim writes, " If any man shall demand of me
how it comes to pass that the diminution, or Differences of arms before mentioned are so diversely
borne, not only in foreign countries, but also in
one self nation, or why there is not one set form
observed in the use of them with all nations, I

answer that it is not possible, because of the infinite actions of men, which are no less infinitely subject to mutability, and therefore can by no means be reduced to a set form of bearing universally." (I have modernised the worthy old herald's spelling out of consideration for the reader's patience.) The same writer defines Differences as being "Extraordinary additaments, whereby bearers of the same coat armour are distinguished each from others, and the nearness to the original bearer is demonstrated." This remark would only apply to the later style of differences, such as the Label, Crescent, &c., before enumerated, and which are now termed "the marks of Cadency."

As regards the other kind of Differences, Boutell's "Heraldry" defines them to consist of such arms as show a "Feudal influence," and this is exhibited by various means, all of which indicate in a greater or less degree the motive which suggested their adoption. He gives an example of the Luttrel arms, which consisted of, Or, a bend between six martlets sable, which was differenced by other families to mark their feudal alliance with the house of Luttrel. The De Furnivals bore the shield of Luttrel with a change of colour, viz. argent, a bend between six martlets gules. *Their* feudal allies or dependants differenced these arms amongst themselves, as the De Wadeslies bore De Furnival's coat with three escallops Or on the bend. The De Wortleys bore the same coat with three bezants on the bend, in place of the escallops. The De Mounteneys bore, sable a bend between six martlets Or. Among the De Mounteneys there was a further difference for Cadency in the various branches of the family. Instead of gules, Sir Ernulph de Mounteney has the field of his escutcheon azure, his bend and martlets Or. Sir John has the same arms, but charges his bend with a *mullet* gules. These arms were probably personally assumed by their various bearers, and not conferred by king or herald. Doubtless he whose arms were imitated consented to such action as a special mark of esteem and gratitude.

The Border, both plain and charged, is a mark of Cadency, and has been borne by princes as well as by others of various ranks. It usually marks the eldest branch of a large and flourishing family.

Planché says as to Differences, or Brizures as they are sometimes called, "No general rule having been laid down, it is probable that the Differences were assumed according to the fancy of the bearer or prevailing fashion of the period, advised perhaps occasionally, or sanctioned, by a competent officer of arms." The illustrious Camden, of whom Spenser appears unable to fully express his admiration, adds some interesting details as to feudal influences in coat armour. In his "Remaines" he writes, "About this time did many gentlemen begin to bear arms by borrowing those of their lords, of whom they held their fees, or to whom they were most devoted, so that, whereas the Earls of Chester bore three garbs or wheat-sheaves (of gold, in a field of azure), many gentlemen of that county took wheat-sheaves. The old Earl of Warwick bore chequie Or and azure, a chevron ermine, so many thereabout took ermine and chequie. In Leicestershire many bore cinquefoils, for that the ancient Earls of Leicester bore gules a cinquefoil ermine. In Westmorland the old barons of Kendal bore argent, two bars gules, and a lion passant Or in a Canton gules, so many gentlemen thereabout took the same, in different colours and charges in the canton." In Cornwall the duke's arms were, sable, fifteen bezants, and consequently many families in that duchy bore bezants in their arms. Camden also states that, in the time of warlike expeditions, gentlemen of blood would repair to the Earl Marshal and by his authority take arms, which were registered by the officers in the Rolls of Arms, made at every expedition, of which several still remain, such as those made at the siege of Caerlaverock, the battle of Stirling, the siege of Calais, and at various tournaments.

Guillim tells us of yet another form of differencing. He says, "Before differencing by means of labels, crescents, mullets, &c., was devised, a gentleman being a younger brother used to adopt two of the coats of arms of his nearest kinsfolk, and marshal them together in one shield, parted *per chevron*," that is, by a line formed like a chevron. This is probably the originating cause of many of the arms of this fashion which we meet with. Regarding all these kinds of Differences, I think there is no cause to doubt that, when first adopted by their assumers, the symbolical meaning of the charges influenced the choice of the assumer, whilst the symbolism of the colours, also, was probably never lost sight of or despised. If heraldry was symbolical, it follows, as a matter of course, that the Differences were also adopted with a symbolical intent, although in a kind of reflected sense, because the admitted existence of the superior or principal arms, owned by another, would imply a desire to copy from him who was worthy of admiration and of imitation.

There is an instance on record, of a herald getting an alteration made in his own paternal arms. Augustine Vincent, Windsor Herald, *temp.* James I., obtained a grant from his brethren at Heralds' College, altering the arms long borne by his ancestors, namely, a blue shield with three white quatrefoils and a border of the latter colour, to the following arms : on a gold shield a blue pile bearing the three white quatrefoils. It should also be noted, that the quatrefoils were borne pierced in the latter coat. The reasons given in the grant are, that the use of the previous coat had been specially confirmed to Vincent's cousin, Mrs. Johanne Mulsho, and he therefore wished to "betake himself to some kind of Difference which might distinguish him and his posterity from the said ancient and elder house." ("Memoir of Vincent," by Sir Harris Nicolas.)

From all these various customs of differencing, it arises that in many instances of coats of arms that have come down to us from ancient times, we are only able to speculate whether such arms may be original or differenced coats, and if the latter, then as to the original coats from which they were derived.

We must not, however, be discouraged with heraldry because of these doubts and difficulties. Like our language — and even the human race itself—it has to bear its traces of changeful growth, and of sometimes ill-judged selection, while the absence of written rule and order in ancient times, has left it to us to-day to take heraldry at its best, as a memorial of a romantic past, as well as of our brave forefathers who sleep their sleep, and the fruit of whose good works we now enjoy.

INDEX

THE END

Printed by BALLANTYNE, HANSON & CO.
Edinburgh & London

Printed in the United States
129833LV00001B/63/A

9 780766 141681